# GRANT WRITER'S HANDBOOK

For Successful Public Safety Grant Proposals

A 5-Step Process & Toolkit to Achieve State & Local Grant Success Goals

By:

Kurt Bradley

Margaret Stark

Don Philpott

Published by
Homeland Defense Grants ™
www.HDGrants.com

Grant Writer's Handbook

### About the Publisher – Government Training Inc. ™

Homeland Defense Grants is a business unit of Government Training, Inc. and is a full service grant consulting firm, serving the needs of the First Responder and Public Safety Agency community. We specialize in providing project development, writing and/or reviewing grants, and training of grant professionals working within the public safety and first responder sector. www.GovernmentTrainingInc.com

We have been serving the grant development needs of law enforcement, fire, EMS, and emergency management agencies across the country. Our clients have a 78% funding success rate. Our success rate is directly attributable to our industry specific focus.

We understand that many of you are working with very tight budgets and that your time is extremely limited and valuable. Let us help you learn to obtain the funding you need to stretch your budgets, increase officer safety, and get the equipment you need to do your job safely and effectively.

Copyright © 2010 Government Training Inc.

All rights reserved. Printed in the United States of America. This publication is protected by copyright, and permission must be obtained from the publisher prior to any prohibited reproduction, storage in a retrieval system or transmission in any form or by any means, electronic, mechanical, photocopying, recording or likewise. For information regarding permissions, write to:

Government Training Inc. ™
Rights and Contracts Department
5372 Sandhamn Place
Longboat Key, Florida 34228
Don.dickson@GovernmentTrainingInc.com
ISBN: 978-0-9844038-0-6

The authors, through their combined 30 years of actual and relevant experience, have performed extensive research and analysis to bring the reader the first and most comprehensive desk reference available on successfully developing, applying and winning grant funding targeted specifically for First Responder and Public Safety Agencies. The book is designed and targeted specifically at the common public safety or first responder employee offering them a comprehensive, yet easily understood guide, to understanding, developing applying and successfully winning grant funding from the Department of Homeland Security and other Federal, State, Corporate and Private Foundation funding sources.

# Contents

Grant Writer's Handbook .................................................................................................. i

Foreword .......................................................................................................................... 1

**1. Introduction** ............................................................................................................. 5
    *Find and Train The Right Person* .................................................................................. 5
    *So, Exactly What Is A Grant?* ....................................................................................... 7
    *Funding Sources* ............................................................................................................ 9
    *Types Of Grants* .......................................................................................................... 12

**2: Critical Infrastructure** ........................................................................................ 17
    *What Is Critical Infrastructure And Why Do You Need To Know About It?* ............. 17

**3. Step One: The Basics** ........................................................................................... 33
    *Proper Grant Strategy* ................................................................................................. 33
    *Forming A Grants Team* ............................................................................................. 35
    *DUNS (DUNS Universal Numbering System) Number* ............................................ 41
    *NIMS (National Incident Management System) Compliance* .................................... 43
    *Finding Funding* ......................................................................................................... 45
    *The Politics Of Grants* ................................................................................................ 54

**4. Step Two: You Found A Grant** ......................................................................... 57
    *Reviewing Request For Proposal (Rfp)/Guidelines* ................................................... 57

**5. Step Three: The Grant Proposal** ...................................................................... 75
    *Components of a Grant* .............................................................................................. 75
    *Project Summary* ........................................................................................................ 76
    *Problem/Needs Statement* .......................................................................................... 79
    *Program Approach/Project Description* ..................................................................... 90
    *Financial Need* .......................................................................................................... 100
    *Cost Benefit* .............................................................................................................. 108
    *Goals and Objectives* ................................................................................................ 120
    *Evaluation* ................................................................................................................. 124
    *Performance Measures/Evaluation* ........................................................................... 127
    *Establishing Performance Indicators* ....................................................................... 130
    *Timeline Management Plan* ..................................................................................... 132
    *Sustainability* ............................................................................................................ 137
    *Exportable Products* ................................................................................................. 140
    *Budget* ...................................................................................................................... 145

www.HDGrants.com

Grant Writer's Handbook

**6. Step Four: Alternative Funding** ............................................. 153
*Corporate/Private Foundation Solicitations* .................................. 153
*Alternative Funding Strategies* ............................................... 166
*Think Training Aid, Not Equipment* ........................................... 173
*20: Proposal Format* ......................................................... 176

**7. Grant Writing Tips** ........................................................ 179

**8. Step Five: After the Application Process** ................................ 183
*"Congratulations, Your Grant Is Approved"* ................................... 183
*Checklist Of Common Reasons Grants Get Declined* ............................. 190

**9. Wrap Up** ................................................................. 197

## About the authors

### Kurt T. Bradley

Kurt T. Bradley is the Vice President of Homeland Defense Grants. He served in the USAF and upon being honorably discharged, began a 26- year career in law enforcement. He was a certified law enforcement instructor with the State of Florida and the grant writer for his city. He served on the regional FBI Anti-terrorist task force after the events of 9-11. Upon retiring as a police administrator he became the grant manager for the local Housing Authority writing to HUD and corporate and private foundations for social service programs. Kurt's work there resulted in several national "Best Practice" recognition awards from HUD. In 2004, he was appointed director of CHIEF Grants (a business unit of CHIEF Corp) responsible for developing and providing grant writing training and grant development services to public safety agencies nationwide. He has assisted public safety agencies win more than $165 million dollars in grant awards from corporate/private foundations, local, state, and federal grant programs. Kurt is a regularly published journalist and has been a featured guest columnist for the Homeland Defense Journal, Police Fleet Magazine, Wildland Firefighter, JEMS, Campus safety Magazine and other public safety publications. His broad range of experience in public safety, grant writing, and journalism makes him uniquely qualified to handle the needs of public safety agencies and others. Kurt brings a unique perspective to this field both as a former agency "administrator-in-need" and as a grant professional. His experience will serve your department well as you compete for the billions of dollars in grant monies available through the Department of Homeland Security and other public and private sources of grant funding. Kurt has attained certifications with the National Grant Writers Association as a Certified Grants Consultant, Certified Grants Reviewer, Certified Grants Administrator, Senior Certified Grants Specialist, and Certified Grants Specialist.

### Margaret Stark

Margaret Stark is a public safety grant specialist, providing grants services for Homeland Defense Grants. Margaret Stark was the law enforcement grant specialist for ITT Industries Night Vision since 1998, CHIEF Grants since 2004, TASER since 2008, PoliceGrantsHelp.com since 2008, and L-3 Com since 2009. Margaret has been published in professional publications for law enforcement such as Homeland Defense Journal, Police Magazine, Air Beat Magazine, Law and Order Magazine, as well as on PoliceOne.com to name just a few. She is responsible for personally assisting thousands of police departments across the US and directing their efforts and applications for funding to obtain Federal, State, and Foundation/Private funding totaling well over $150 million. She was previously employed with the Pulaski Police Department in VA, and was the grant writer/administrator for that department during her tenure. She has an additional five years experience in writing grants and fund raising for nonprofits as well. She is an accomplished speaker and instructor, and has presented grant-writing training at national and regional conferences for the past ten years such as the International Association of Chiefs of Police (IACP) annual conference, the American Society for Law Enforcement Trainers (ASLET)

annual conference, Virginia Chief's Association, The Performance Institute, and Sigarms Academy, University of Virginia Command College, Airborne Law Enforcement Association (ALEA), Congressman Steven LaTourette Annual Conference, TREXPO East and West as well as various other academies and law enforcement facilities across the U.S. Margaret is a certified by the National Grant Writers Association as Senior Grants Specialist, Grant Consultant, Grant Administrator, and Grant Evaluator.

### Don Philpott

Don Philpott is editor of International Homeland Security, a quarterly journal for homeland security professionals, and has been writing, reporting and broadcasting on international events, trouble spots and major news stories for more than 40 years. For 20 years he was a senior correspondent with Press Association -Reuters, the wire service, and traveled the world on assignments including Northern Ireland, Lebanon, Israel, South Africa and Asia.

He writes for magazines and newspapers in the United States and Europe and is a contributor to radio and television programs on security and other issues. He is the author of more than 90 books on a wide range of subjects and has had more than 5,000 articles printed in publications around the world. His most recent books are Terror - Is America Safe?, The Wounded Warrior Handbook, The Workplace Violence Prevention Handbook, and Public School Emergency Preparedness and Crisis Management. He is a member of the National Press Club.

# FOREWORD

Welcome to the world of grants for public safety agencies. Are you tired of seeing the budget axe swung at your department's funding year after year? Are you fed up with using "hand-me-downs" from other agencies and being told to "make do with what you have?" Is your equipment older than you are? Are you sick and tired of hearing "maybe in next year's budget" from your top administrators? Then it is time for your department to learn about the billions of dollars in grants that are available for your use, every year in the United States.

At some point in time, we all must realize that our tax bases, from which we draw our salaries and operating budgets, are shrinking at an alarming rate. Taxpayers, of whom you are also one, can only afford to fund just so many tax increases year after year. If they are not already doing so, eventually they will start saying, "enough is enough"! These words are the bane of every public safety agency in the United States. Let's face it; if your town or city is not growing, then neither is your tax base.

Although you may have experienced significant growth during the last ten years, the projected growth for the future is not so promising given our country's current economic condition. Yet, your annual calls for service are steadily increasing and in many cases, the tax dollars needed to support additional personnel, vehicles, new office space, and equipment has not kept pace with the demand for these services. Money simply to operate our departments has become frequently scarce. Where is this money supposed to come from for the increased salaries, step-pay plans, new vehicles, and new, state-of-the-art equipment?

Public Safety Agencies across the United States are now being tasked to do more with less. It takes money to fight criminals and terrorists who are endowed with seemingly unlimited supplies of money and who routinely outspend us 10-1 on technological advances. So what is your department to do? One solution is to use grant-funding streams!

Every year in this country there is $100+ billion dollars in Federal, State, Local, Foundation/Corporate, and private grants available for these purposes. Money for equipment, personnel, and programs to fight or defend the safety and sanctity of our way of life is there for your use. It has always been there, sometimes less than at other times, but the programs have existed for decades to assist you in your missions. New grant programs open on a regular basis, but this information often remains obscured from your normal everyday agendas. After

## Grant Writer's Handbook

all, the task of grant writing to the average public safety employee is usually just "another duty as assigned".

So, why are so many departments not getting this money every year? The answer is decidedly simple. Grants are like the lottery; "if you don't play, you can't win!" It is that simple. Many of you reading this have probably tried to write a grant at sometime, only to receive the dreaded rejection notice or "Dear John" letter. It is never easy to accept rejection especially for a public safety employee. We work in a very machismo type job and saying "no" to one of us, is usually a certain ride to the local lockup. We don't take rejection well at all, as it stifles our desire to forge forward and try again. You may have decided that it is not worth your time to read and re-read an RFP (request for proposal) that is 80 pages long, just to find out if you can get a box of pens for free.

Admit it! Most of us in this profession do not have English majors or degrees in creative writing. You are "adrenaline junkies;" who would rather be out "cuffing and stuffing", "putting wet stuff on the red stuff" or "saving lives" than spending hours researching, reading, and writing a grant. We know you do not have hours of idle free time sitting around to research, apply for and manage a grant. This is understandable and the authors have experienced your pain as well.

This book is presented in language that you, as a public safety official, will understand and is based upon the experiences and education of two of the country's top public safety grant consultants. That knowledge and experience has resulted in millions of dollars in grant awards to agencies, just like yours, across the United States. This book is the benefit of those years of experience and the miles that the authors have walked in your shoes. So get ready to learn what it takes to be a winner in this "grants ballgame". There are rules, playbooks, and team members. Those who play closest to the rules, usually win.

## Symbols

Throughout this book you will see a number of icons displayed in the margins. The icons are there to help you as you work through the Five Step process. Each icon acts as an advisory – for instance alerting you to things that you must always do or should never do. The icons used are:

**Must Do**     This is something that you must always do

**No No**     This is something you should never do

**Tips**     Really useful tips

**Remember**     Points to bear in mind

**Checklist**     Have you checked off or answered everything on this list before you submit your application?

Grant Writer's Handbook

# 1. Introduction

### Find and Train The Right Person

The first step for any organization to take in deciding to participate in grants, is to recognize that it takes a specific type of person to accomplish this task. Grants require a great deal of reading and comprehension and the ability to stay organized and focused on the task. It is, therefore, essential to properly choose and train the right person in your organization who will be developed into the "grants specialist."

The person you choose should possess most if not all of the following skills:

- ☐ **Organizational skills** – grant proposals are highly organized documents. There is paperwork that must be placed in order, documents that will need to be written and tracked and reporting requirements that must be met in a timely fashion. This requires that the person being placed in charge of these tasks be organized themselves, in order to comply with timelines, reporting requirements and deadlines.

- ☐ **Communication skills** – From the first day that you signed on as a public safety employee you had to learn to communicate effectively with the public, your peers and amongst yourselves. We all "speak the language" when it comes to radio communications. A good grant writer learns to communicate those verbal skills into the written word. Grant writing is nothing more than being an effective story teller. The task is very similar to being a photo-journalist where the photographer's eye and camera capture an image and relay that image and its feeling and impact to the viewer in a visual format. A grant must essentially do the same thing, It is a snapshot of the working environment and community that you live and work in, being related in 10 minutes or less to someone who has never seen or heard anything about you or your community and department. Failed grants typically present a black and white photograph, where a good grant writer delivers an 8X10, color glossy, 15 megapixel photo clearly showing the problem and a solution.

- ☐ **Ability to focus**- It is essential that a grant writer stay focused on the task at hand. A grant has to present a reasoned and well thought out plan to the reviewer in order to

www.HDGrants.com

receive a funding award. If you are easily distracted, you will leave out critical details that must be included as part of a truly comprehensive and well planned project.

- ☐ **Technical report writing skills** – This is a basic skill that all effective public safety employees should already possess. Our profession requires and demands good, accurate reports to be written and filed on the incidents that we respond to. If you have been a public safety employee for any length of time you probably already possess this skill or have been placed through some remediation training to improve this ability.

- ☐ **Thinking "Outside the Box"** – This is probably the single biggest skill that a successful grant writer can possess. Grant writing is all about new and unique ideas. A good grant application always presents a unique solution, to a unique problem for a unique community. This is a task where your imagination can run wild as you envision a better, safer, or more efficient way for getting the job done. Grant writing is similar to being in Research & Development at a big private company. Do it better, faster, longer with less tools, spending less money and getting a large "bang for the buck" are the calls to duty. Being able to step outside the traditional way of doing things and see things from a different perspective of "what if" is a big plus. Dreamers with active imaginations do well in this field. It is encouraged.

- ☐ **Ability to work unsupervised** – If you are the type of person who has to have someone cracking the whip over your head at all times to motivate you, you will not do well in this field. Grant writing is for the most part a solitary task. It is a thought process whereby random ideas are analyzed and discarded; disorder is placed into order and then transferred from brain to paper. It is usually best accomplished in quiet places with deep reflection and forethought before placing pen to paper. It requires a person that is a self-starter and deeply motivated to succeed. You do not need a supervisor standing over your shoulder, mucking up your thought process or causing you to stray from program priorities, goals, and objectives that having never read and comprehended the RFP, they would know nothing about.

- ☐ **Punctuality** – There is a single rule in grant writing that all grant writers must never violate. Grant deadlines are chiseled in stone. Miss a deadline and $250K in badly needed funding is gone for a full year and probably, so is your job as a grant writer. Punctuality is not a recommended virtue here, it is an absolute necessity!

- ☐ **Computer Literacy** – Grant writing requires research and knowledge beyond your local work environment. The advent of modern computers and availability of the Internet to grant writers was similar in scope with what the invention of automobiles was to horse and buggy days. Twenty-some years ago grant writing research literally took months to accomplish because all the research had to be done by hand, mail or

# Introduction

in person investigation. You needed an army of workers to collect and collate all the information that was needed in a grant application to get funded. Those same tasks today are performed with a mouse click from the comfort of your Lazy-Boy and within seconds of your question, you have an answer. It will not be long, as a result of the Federal Paperwork Reduction Act, that all Federal grant applications will have to be filed electronically.

The above listed skills and traits can help you identify who might be the most logical choice for assigning the task of grant writing. Remember, desire and willingness to do the job will always be a deciding factor in choosing the right person.

Once this person is identified, you must provide them with the proper tools to perform the task, including formalized grant writer development training. This book is a good, comprehensive first start but should not be interpreted as the sole source for providing that training and those skill sets. Seeking out professional advice and training should be a continual and ongoing quest.

## *So, Exactly What Is A Grant?*

If you are the prospective grant writer it makes sense to understand exactly what a grant is, where this money comes from and why it is being given away.

*"A form of gift that entails certain obligations on the part of the grantee and Expectations on the part of the grantor"* Dorsey Dictionary

In good old plain English a grant is a monetary award to perform certain deeds or services and achieve certain goals and objectives to solve a unique, particular problem in your agency and community. But just exactly where does this money they give away come from? A grant maker, or funding source, needs to be thought of more or less as a bank in which money is collected and then distributed.

In the case of a Federal grant program the money collected comes from the taxes that you and I pay every year. From some of those taxes, money is distributed to various public agencies that use that money to build roads and bridges, pay for education, fund health care research and health care programs and other social service type programs. This is how all of these things get built within our communities or paid for. In the case of public safety agencies in the U.S., these tax dollars go to organizations such as the Department of Justice, National Institute for Justice, Bureau of Justice Assistance, Federal Emergency Management Agency, U.S. Fire Administration, Centers for Disease Control, and a myriad of other organizations.

Grant Writer's Handbook

That money is then apportioned to states and the trickledown effect begins on getting that money into the hands of local government agencies of which you are a part.

In the case of a private, community or corporate funding source the money is typically collected from wealthy or philanthropic individuals and pooled together, as in the case of Community Foundations or non-profit groups to whom private citizens and businesses donate. Corporate entities collect the dollars they will give away from the company profits and this money is then channeled into their charitable giving arms or foundations. The primary reason for all this giving by these groups is quite simple; they receive a tax break from the IRS for doing so. There is certainly a "sympathy factor" here in wanting to "do good in our community" but quite frankly, most people who donate and/or companies who have charitable foundations they support are doing so to garner better public relations and they use it as a marketing tool and tax break option. The overriding theme of corporate and private foundations in their giving rests in "improving the human condition" be that through education, social, service programs, health, and economic improvement.

How do you think new tools are developed - that improve efficiency or devise new and safer techniques for dealing with crime? Grant makers are always looking for the "easy replication factor" in your programs. In other words, can another agency easily do the same thing and expect to achieve the same results? They want to see new cost-effective ways of dealing with problems. Some examples of these programs are Crime Prevention Officers, Neighborhood Watch Programs, Community Oriented Policing, DARE and Fire Prevention and Safety Programs. All of these grant programs were started as the result of a grant program that demonstrated a new idea and this idea worked or improved efficiency and achieved the result sought. The results of the evaluations of those programs provided the basis for taking this program to other agencies in the hopes of achieving similar results. This is important to know if you expect to be successful at approaching grant funding sources. The results that they are seeking in order to give away the money in the first place usually revolved around:

- ☐ cost effective and saved money
- ☐ easily replicated by others who would achieve the same results
- ☐ resulted in a safer or more efficient means to accomplish something

In other words life got better and easier for the citizens or those performing the tasks for those citizens.

Every agency has needs, but grantors are typically interested in funding projects that will serve a large audience of citizens for a greater good, benefit the community, provide additional

www.HDGrants.com

## Introduction

safety or reduce or eliminate a problem. This is often referred to as "cost benefit" or "bang for their buck." When you write a grant application, you must "think" the problem through thoroughly. Just as a bank will ask for a "business plan" before lending you money to open a business, a grantor will want to know what your game plan is. That is why grants are mostly "competitive" in nature. Grantors will give the best and most comprehensive plans, the most consideration.

The grantor will request reasonable assurances from you, before awarding you the grant. These include:

- ☐ That you indeed have a unique problem facing your department and community
- ☐ That this problem was studied thoroughly and you can provide statistical data to support your contention that a problem actually exists.
- ☐ That you have explored other financial options attempting to resolve the problem on your own.
- ☐ You have determined that you do not or will not have the available financial resources to deal with this problem.
- ☐ That you have carefully mapped out a comprehensive solution to the problem.
- ☐ That if awarded, you can achieve your stated goals.
- ☐ That you have an alternative plan in the event your original plan does not succeed.

Checklist

Unlike a bank that would expect repayment of a loan, a grant is a gift, you will not have to pay it back in most cases. It is not ,therefore, unreasonable for a funding source or grantor, to expect that you be a good steward of this money and show that you have a comprehensive plan laid out, before granting you an award. As the recipient of a grant or "gift" you will be expected to provide reports that will prove that you are working within the stated goals of the RFP. These reports will show your progress and grade you on your success with the grant or funding.

## Funding Sources

### 1. Federal Funding

On average approximately $65 billion in funding is available every year for various programs from the Federal government.

# Grant Writer's Handbook

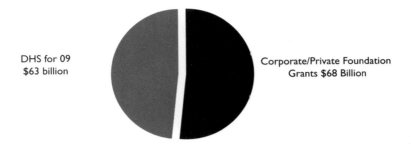

DHS for 09
$63 billion

Corporate/Private Foundation
Grants $68 Billion

You might be thinking, if these Federal grants are so available, why haven't I heard about them before? The reason you have not heard about them is simple! The government does not do a very good job of marketing these opportunities, nor do they readily advertise the availability of grant programs through the modern day primary sources of our everyday knowledge base; television, newspaper and the Internet. You must know where to look.

Even though this information is public record--unless you are well informed of the process and the funding sources out there--it can quickly become an un-navigable quagmire to try to collate all the data that does exist in so many different places. The government, during the last several years, has made some drastic improvements to make this process easier, which we will discuss later.

For those who do happen to hear about the programs, they often find it difficult to locate the right office, cannot get all the necessary information, fail to properly interpret or translate the RFP (request for proposal) and find that there are so many programs that not even the government employees themselves know all the proper procedures to follow!

## 2. State/Local Funding

A large majority of the Federal funding available each year, passes down directly to the State level where it is apportioned to local municipalities and local governments. In most cases, if you are dealing with Department of Homeland Security monies, the ONLY way you will have access to those funds is through your State Administering Agency.

There are many grant programs offered in each of the states and new programs are offered every year. However, it seems that the states are just not very efficient at getting the word out to the agencies that could apply. It is not surprising, therefore, that most people have no idea of the millions of dollars that are available from the states. The thousands of different programs and the varying dates for application and qualification processes make it that much more difficult to understand exactly how to obtain this money.

## Introduction

### 3. Foundation Funding

☐ Corporate Funding

☐ Private Giving

Over 1.1 million grants awarded totaling $68.6 billion is available every year from Corporate and Private Foundations.

A Foundation is a nonprofit organization, many times part of a large for-profit company, whose main purpose is to improve society's ills. Each foundation has its own special field of interest, and if you meet the eligibility requirements and can match your need with their giving priorities, you can receive a cash grant.

---

**Must Do**

The eligibility requirements you most often see for foundation grants is the IRS nonprofit status designation of 501c3, or being designated as a local government agency. If the funder states they will only fund 501c3 organizations, you may have to look for a partner that in fact has this status to apply to this foundation if your organization does not hold that IRS designation itself. There are many 501c3 groups in your community and most are more than willing to assist in a program that will benefit the community. Another approach that has proven successful for many agencies across the country is to form a 501c3 organization themselves. This is not uncommon for local volunteer Fire Departments or Rescue Squads to use. One manifestation of the company's concern for good citizenship is the philanthropic contributions they make around the world. Not only is it appropriate for these companies and foundations to give back to the communities in which they operate, it is also smart business for two reasons. Healthy communities are important to the well-being of society and the overall economy and most for-profit companies get a considerable tax break for making these donations.

---

Most of these companies fund interests involved in education, child welfare, community development, and economic growth. It might seem that these funding priorities would not align with a public safety agency however; if you look between the lines and "think outside the box", you will quickly discover how to form that nexus between your needs and theirs. That, my friend, is the key to grant writing success.

Recognizing that you must first meet the funding source's priorities and make your project align with their philosophy is the key to receiving an award. Simply put, it is their money and if you want their money, you have to play by their rules!

Believe us when we say that these foundations are literally seeking you out, so that they can give this money away. Otherwise, they face losing the tax advantage that giving this money away offers to them.

These Corporate and Private Foundation entities, by law, must give away a percentage of their income or profits every year to utilize the tax advantage extended to them by the

www.HDGrants.com

# Grant Writer's Handbook

IRS.. The parent companies of these foundations need the tax advantages offered to them for funneling some of their profits into a nonprofit foundation. The nonprofit foundation then offers the money, for various funding interests as grants, and both the nonprofit and the parent company end up reaping the public relations benefits, not to mention a significant tax advantage.

It also serves them another purpose that is especially of interest to public safety agencies. Have you ever thought about how much money you spend in your lifetime? You might be surprised to know that the figure for an average American has been estimated, according to several Internet resources, to be about $2.5 million dollars. Since we "save those lives" we are preserving economic security for those companies, on some scale, who rely on those citizens being alive and well and spending money in their stores buying things. HHHHMMMMH! Does it make sense to help those you help save lives, you betcha! One only has to put forward a train of thought along the lines of something like, 4 lives lost in a residential house fire or bad car accident equals $10 million in potential earning not being spent buying their products. To any business man, saving the lives of their customers and or workers that live in these communities makes financial sense.

These Corporate and Private Foundations are also interested in programs that will "stop losses". If there are situations in your community that are causing these entities to lose money or pay out on claims or higher insurance premiums they are most likely willing to invest in a program that will stop their losses.

Remember: If you think that it is impossible to get free money, let me tell you. It is not impossible, it's a fact! Agencies just like yours and businesses all across the country are receiving millions from these programs without ever having to pay this money back!

## Types Of Grants

### Competitive

These types of grants "compete" with others for being the most worthy of funding. This is where the terminology of being "needy not greedy" and words "make them bleed, make them cry" have the most significance. You must compete against other agencies who also want this money. Your argument (or application) must compel the reviewer to believe that your need is the greatest and most worthy of funding.

These grants of Federal, State, or Local money will have a posted date and a deadline for receiving applications or a notice of intent to apply. Foundation grants typically will ask for a

# Introduction

"letter of inquiry" or a "concept paper" to be submitted for initial screening purposes. They will then come back to the "best of the best" and ask for complete applications and program descriptions.

Once submitted, a panel will score the grant applications using previously established criteria set out by the funding agency. The highest score wins based on the components of your program and how well you adhere or align with those criteria from the RFP (request for proposal). The money for these types of programs is then usually distributed from the highest scoring application to the lowest scoring application until the funding source has expended all of its existing grant funding.

## Discretionary

These grants permit the federal government, according to specific legislation, to exercise judgment or "discretion" in selecting the project or proposal to be supported and in selecting the recipient organization through a competitive process. These funding opportunities usually have less stringent guidelines and criteria for applying.

A discretionary grant program awards funds to the applicant based upon a competitive process. The funding source reviews applications, in part through a formal review process and in light of the legislative and regulatory requirements and published selection criteria established for that program. The review process gives the funding source the discretion to determine which applications best address the program requirements and are, therefore, most worthy of funding.

The National Institute of Justice frequently uses this type of grant for their funding opportunities. They are the research and development arm of law enforcement and are constantly seeking new and improved ways to combat crime. Therefore, they wish to maintain some level of control over allowing funding to go to projects that they feel have the greatest chance of achieving success.

Discretionary grants and cooperative agreements ( see below) support the following types of projects:

- ☐ **Demonstration Projects:** A project to establish or demonstrate the feasibility of new methods or types of services.
- ☐ **Research Projects:** A project to develop new knowledge or to evaluate existing knowledge in new settings.

- ☐ **Training Projects:** A project to support the increase in the number of personnel trained in techniques pertaining to delivering services or performing functions necessary to the development of such services.
- ☐ **Service Projects:** A project to support the cost of developing, organizing, establishing, providing or expanding the delivery of services.
- ☐ **Construction Projects:** A project to support the building or expansion of a facility.
- ☐ **Fellowship or Scholarships:** A discretionary grant providing direct support to the education of one or more students in a specific discipline.

## Block/Formula

These are grants that the Federal agency has been directed by Congress to make to grantees, for which the limits of funding amount is established by a mathematical formula based on criteria that are written into the legislation and program regulations This funding is directly awarded and administered in the Federal agency's program offices.

In other words, the federal government will use a certain statistical figure (UCR Index Crimes for example) weighed against the population of the State to determine just how much of the overall money appropriated for the program goes to each State or local agency.

This is how Federal money is apportioned to the States and then distributed to local agencies.

The State will in most cases apply a similar type formula to determine how much of the State's overall share goes to each eligible local jurisdiction.

## Mandatory Grant

Mandatory grants are those that a Federal agency is required by statute to award if the recipient, usually a State, submits an acceptable State Plan or application, and meets the eligibility and compliance requirements of the statutory and regulatory provisions of the grant program. In the past, mandatory grants were sometimes referred to as "formula grants." Mandatory grants include block, open-ended and closed-ended grants.

**Block Grant:** This is a mandatory grant where the recipients, normally States, have substantial authority over the type of activities to support and with minimal Federal administrative restrictions. The basic premise is that States should be free to target resources and design administrative mechanisms to provide services to best meet the needs of their citizens. Some examples of block grants would be:

- ☐ Community Development Block Grants

# Introduction

☐ Local Law Enforcement Block Grants

**Open-Ended Grant:** This is a mandatory grant where there is no upper limit on the amount of funds the Federal government will pay for allowable services and activities. The principal entitlement grants of the Social Security Act are: 1) Child Support Enforcement and Establishment of Paternity, 2) Foster Care and Adoption Assistance, and 3) Medical Assistance (Medicaid).

**Closed-Ended Grant:** A type of mandatory grant where the award constitutes an upper limit on the amount of funds the Federal government may pay for the activities, hence "closed-ended."

## Cooperative Agreements

☐ A type of Federal assistance; essentially, a variation of a discretionary grant, awarded by a Federal agency when it anticipates having substantial involvement with the grantee during the performance of a funded project.

☐ An agreement between the funding source and the agency, with stipulations that they will provide certain levels of assistance in exchange for you providing certain things as well.

Cooperative agreements are also considered to be the Research & Development type grants where new technologies are being sought or more efficient/safer methods of delivering services are tried.

This is where technologies such as Kevlar for soft body armor got their start and allowed DuPont to develop the specific Kevlar fiber used in those bulletproof vests that law enforcement and the U.S. Military now uses. This initial cooperative agreement between NIJ and DuPont led to the development of the Bulletproof Vest Partnership Program grant that is now offered yearly through the Bureau of Justice Assistance.

The performance periods may be multi-year in nature and there will be close oversight of the grant project by the Federal agency issuing the grant.

These are the only grants where failure is not such an awfully bad thing to occur as the government is usually trying to gauge the effectiveness of the project. If they can learn that this method does not work, it saves them throwing more good money after bad.

At the conclusion of most cooperative agreements, the grantee will be required to develop a white paper for publication in a trade magazine detailing the project either as a success or failure. The funding source usually provides assistance in accomplishing this.

## Congressional Earmarks Or "Pork" Projects

Earmarks or "pork" projects consist of funds handed directly to an agency or community without any of the competitive process. To obtain these funds agencies will, almost always, involve a political process.

This is where you would use your US Congressional representatives to plead your case and obtain funding that might have been denied or is needed for that really special project that just has to be funded in your district.

These earmarks usually get added into some long, obscure bill seeking appropriations for a specific reason and being placed before our Congress. They are sometimes attached to bills in the "11th hour" and pushed through Congress in an effort to escape close scrutiny

Earmarked projects are usually recognized in our communities by seeing the name of a Congressman on a bridge or school house plaque or a new highway that was named after the Congressional representative who obtained the funding.

# 2: CRITICAL INFRASTRUCTURE

## What Is Critical Infrastructure And Why Do You Need To Know About It?

The reason for the creation of the Department of Homeland Security – and its mission - is to "protect the critical infrastructure of the United States". As such, it stands to reason that if the funding stream is coming from DHS, that it should be directed towards accomplishing that goal.

---

Critical Infrastructure as defined by the Department of Homeland Security is defined in Presidential Executive Order 13228. Most DHS grants are predicated on the basis of risk and "risk" is directly tied to what "critical infrastructure" is within your area of responsibility. In order to obtain funding from a federal DHS program it is essential that you always list what "critical infrastructure" is in your areas and stating that you have responsibility for this infrastructure as a first responder.

---

**Executive Order 13228.** Following the terror attacks of September 11, 2001, President Bush signed new Executive Orders relating to critical infrastructure protection. Executive Order 13228, signed October 8, 2001, established the Office of Homeland Security and the Homeland Security Council. Among the duties assigned, the Office was to coordinate efforts to protect:

- ☐ Energy production, transmission / distribution services, and critical facilities
- ☐ Other utilities
- ☐ Telecommunications
- ☐ Facilities that produce, use, store, or dispose of nuclear material
- ☐ Public and privately owned information systems
- ☐ Special events of national significance
- ☐ Transportation, including railways, highways, shipping ports and waterways
- ☐ Airports and civilian aircraft
- ☐ Livestock, agriculture, and systems for the provision of water and food for human use and consumption.

www.HDGrants.com

Critical Infrastructure can also be defined as being any asset that if destroyed or compromised would cause catastrophic loss of life or serious economic disruption.

When you are writing a narrative statement for a DHS grant, it is important to list these "critical infrastructure" concerns and to do so quite clearly. When assessing your critical infrastructure, that is present locally, one of the best ways to do this is to get out of the driver's seat of your department vehicle and have someone drive you through your areas of responsibility. Get your eyes off the road ahead and start paying closer attention to what you see off the roadway and in the distance and then investigate it more thoroughly.

How many times have you been driving through town and stopped at a stop sign only to see a sign posted that says "Call Here First Before You Dig"; did you ever call to see exactly what was buried down there? Perhaps it was a fiber optic cable that links two major metropolitan areas or a pipeline that serves a major International Airport in the next state.

What about that blinking strobe light you always see out there a few miles off some highway at night. Is that a microwave transmission tower or a public safety radio dispatch antennae? What is being stored in that big white tank up there on that hill? Inquiring minds need to know!

You don't know these things until you ask. There are certain things that simply by their mere explanation, will qualify as critical infrastructure but others must be quantified with supportive data in order for them to be considered as such.

As an example, if you listed that you had a Nuclear Power Plant within 25 miles of you, then that speaks for itself. However, if you stated you had an underground pipeline in your area, unless you stated what it pumps and what its maximum flow capacity is, the reviewer would not know if it is a 2 inch Natural Gas local distribution line or a 72 inch Natural Gas pipeline that traverses the entire US pumping in excess of 3-4 billion cubic feet of Natural Gas daily. There is a huge difference between the two.

**!  Must Do** It is therefore essential, that if you are going to claim critical infrastructure concerns, that you in fact quantify those items that you are going to list. This will allow the reviewers to put your total "perceived and actual risk" in proper perspective.

Now by their very nature critical infrastructure concerns sometimes involve data that is not for general release to the public but, as a local public safety agency with a responsibility for any incident involving it, you do have a right to know. You also need to remember when asking for this information that you should let them know that you are applying to a DHS grant

## Critical Infrastructure

program where you need to identify and quantify all of the critical infrastructure in your area. Most will cooperate; some will be stone walls to you. The point is you must make the effort.

You cannot expect that this information will generally be released to you in a simple phone call to the company; they do not have any way of identifying you or proving that you have a right to know and they will often be reluctant to give that information over the phone. You will usually have to make a written request, addressed to the company headquarters and written on your department's letterhead and signed by the Chief of the department. You may be able to get the information in person, if you appear at their offices in uniform and with proper credentials.

Sometimes they will say that they cannot release the information to you as it is "a matter of National Security" and that is fine. In fact, it is probably the best answer that they could give you. In your grant narrative put down that you attempted to ascertain the capacities of the asset in question however, you were denied that information as a matter of National Security. Frankly, I would rather plant that seed in a reviewer's mind than listing a small pipeline that really might not qualify as critical infrastructure.

This is not information that you will get delivered to you instantly. It may take several weeks to verify that the information can be released before you would receive that data. It is not something that you can do in the final week before a grant deadline; this needs to be accomplished well in advance of a grant application. You can then store the information in a safe place for future use in other applications.

| By doing this it is instantly available for the next grant application and all you will then have to keep track of is any new critical infrastructure as it appears in your areas of responsibility. |  Must Do |

Your "need" for funding, is clearly tied to your actual and perceived risk and responsibilities to these assets and this is one of the ways that you will demonstrate that need.

To give you a better understanding of what they are referring to, in the list above, we have described some of the things that you should be looking for in your area of responsibility. When you are assessing what "critical infrastructure" you have in your area. Compile a list of what is in your primary area and then what is in your mutual aid areas as well.

The logic behind this is simple. By definition, if something happens at a large piece of critical infrastructure, let's say a fire at an Ethanol plant, the chances are that if it is in your mutual aid area you will be called in to provide additional manpower and resources to help mitigate that incident. You would need to be equipped with similar type equipment, just as the

www.HDGrants.com

# Grant Writer's Handbook

primary responding agency, in order to be of any value to them in providing supplementary manpower or providing additional resources.

Remember

Lest we forget, many of the DHS grants are reviewed and read by a "peer panel". What that means is the reviewers reading your application will probably be fellow officers within the same career discipline and as such, you will be trying to affect their thought process. You need to make them see the logic that if they were in the same situation, they would recognize the probability that you would be called in for that assistance and would need to be equipped to handle that task. By doing so, you have elevated your "need" and thereby increased your scoring potential.

Other grants will be sent to your SAA for review prior to peer review and specifically request confirmation that you are working within your state emergency management plan and national emergency response plans. This information can be obtained from your SAA if you don't currently have these plans. Insure that your response to any incident especially regarding the critical infrastructure falls within these plans.

Keep these lists separated and then write three paragraphs, in this order, describing what Critical Infrastructure is in your areas of responsibility;

☐ primary response area, then
☐ what are in your secondary response or mutual aid areas and finally
☐ what is not technically critical infrastructure but, still represents a particular hazard or exposure to your department and citizens.

Let's examine each of the above bullet points and give you a little more insight as to what they are talking about as it relates to what may be in your area.

Sometimes information about a particular item may also be available on the Internet and if you do a "Google search" you may quickly locate the information that you need about that particular asset i.e.; hydroelectric dams and Nuclear Power Plants.

Energy production, transmission, and distribution services and critical facilities – (these items should be part of a regional power grid and carry large amounts or produce large amounts of power so it is important that you indicate how much they handle or produce daily in megawatts)

## Critical Infrastructure

- ☐ Major power generation facilities that exceed 2,000 MW and support the regional electric grid.

- ☐ Electric substations 500 KV or larger, and substations 345 KV or larger, that are part of a critical system supporting populations in excess of one million.

- ☐ High-voltage electrical transmission lines 345 KV or larger

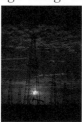

- ☐ Hydroelectric facilities and dams that produce power in excess of 2,000 MgW or could cause catastrophic loss of life if breached.

# Grant Writer's Handbook

- ☐ Pipelines – Buried /Above Ground
    - Should be listed if pumping 1 million gallons per day for liquid products such as petroleum products ( gasoline, diesel, kerosene, jet fuel)
    - Should be listed if pumping 1 billion cubic feet per day capacity for natural gas, chemical gases, propane, LP

- ☐ Refineries
    - What and how much do they store and/or produce daily
    - This can also include propane tank farms or anyplace where there is a large quantity stored

- ☐ Gas or oil well drilling areas w/ daily production or pumping capacities

## Critical Infrastructure

☐ Tank Farms

☐ Solar Panel Farms

☐ Ethanol Production and Storage

☐ Wind Turbines

### Other utilities

☐ Public drinking water systems that serve more than 100K populations

These can include a river or reservoirs that serve multiple cities downstream from you that if you combine those areas populations, they would add up to more than 100K people.

# Grant Writer's Handbook

☐ Aqueducts, canals, pipelines etc. that serve major areas for drinking water

This does not include aquifers or deep wells. They are only concerned with areas where it is conceivable that someone could put biological agents or chemical poisons into them.

### Desalinization plants

☐ Large water treatment plants or sewage treatment plants that serve large populations of more than 100k

### Telecommunications

☐ Large public safety radio transmission towers

☐ Public TV or radio station antennae systems that are part of the Emergency Broadcasting System

☐ Microwave Radio communication towers

## Critical Infrastructure

Large fiber optic cables linking large regional areas or major metropolitan areas that if cut or severed would seriously disrupt either the economic or public safety network.

Telephone switching centers of large capacity or Internet Service Providers (ISPs) linked to large regional or major metropolitan areas (such as Verizon, AOL, EarthLink, Road Runner, etc.)

Facilities that produce, use, store, or dispose of nuclear material

☐ Nuclear power plants within 50- 75 miles of you
- List them even if they are not currently in production or they are planned or under construction

☐ Nuclear or designated Haz-Mat waste dumps
- This may include caves or underground facilities

☐ Irradiation plants
- food irradiation facilities
- medical industries that produce "cancer irradiation products" or use irradiation to sterilize medical instruments

☐ Nuclear fuel rod production facilities
- United States Uranium Enrichment Company facilities
- DOD contractors who fuel nuclear rods or dispose of them for the US military
- Spent uranium ammunition manufacturers

Grant Writer's Handbook

- ☐ Military bases where nuclear war materials are stored or where nuclear powered ships are docked
  - It never hurts to mention ANY active military bases or National Guard facilities that are close to you or in your primary response areas, as these are always considered to be high-risk potential terrorist targets especially if they have nuclear, chemical, or biological WMD on site.

### Public and privately owned information systems

- ☐ Large financial data centers for major bank headquarters or the headquarters for Fortune 500 companies
  - Think Microsoft, Wal-Mart, Sears, Ford, GM, General Foods, Target etc.
  - Think World Trade Center here also
- ☐ Credit card transaction centers for major banking institutions like Wachovia, NationsBank, Chase, American Express, Discover etc.
- ☐ Data storage or record storage facilities
  - Iron Mountain data storage sites
  - Computer centers that run International and National computer systems that link these commercial business to each other

### Special events of national significance

- ☐ They are referring to large public venues where large masses (25K+) of citizens come together at

## Critical Infrastructure

- Sport stadiums of major universities or cities holding more than 50k

- Commercial or Local Convention Centers where more than 50 K might be attending a convention under one roof

- Major amusement parks

- NASCAR or Indy style race tracks

Grant Writer's Handbook

- Pari-mutuel racing tracks of national significance

- National Monuments or National Parks

*Transportation, including railways, highways, shipping ports and waterways*

☐ Interstate, US or State highways linking major metropolitan areas together or that would be "evacuation routes" from these areas

- Always list the average daily traffic count (ADTC) and commercial traffic count from your state DOT
- List the # of miles you cover
- List the number of lanes of traffic
- List what major metropolitan areas they link and or if they are a "designated" evacuation routes from those areas

## Step One: The Basics

- ☐ Bridges over waterways or canyons and valleys that if collapsed would cause serious economic catastrophe or catastrophic loss of life

  - Think Golden Gate, Verrazano Narrows, George Washington, Sunshine Skyway type bridges here when thinking of catastrophic loss of life
  - Smaller bridges for both vehicular and rail traffic if the collapse would cause a catastrophic economic loss such as a major 50-100 mile detour or, serious disruption of public safety

- ☐ Railroads / Rail yards / Intermodal Switching Yards

  - Get the yearly rail car count and haz-mat car count from the railroad and list the # of miles of track in your area

- ☐ Ports

  - These are major ports for commercial ship traffic

Grant Writer's Handbook

Navigable rivers or waterways that have commercial shipping traffic

- Think Mississippi, Missouri, Ohio Rivers etc. where you have barge traffic on them.

### Airports and civilian aircraft

☐ Referring to major airports here that have commercial passenger airline service and or handle commercial cargo terminals in them

- You need to state the name of the airport, distance to it from you, how many passengers they handle a year and how many tons of cargo pass through it a year
- This would definitely include military air bases

Livestock, agriculture, and systems for the provision of water and food for human use and consumption

☐ Think agro-terrorism here

- Major food production facilities
- Grain storage facilities
- Fertilizer plants or production and storage facilities

# Critical Infrastructure

- Livestock feed yards or slaughter houses

Generally speaking the more of these things you list, the more "need" is expressed so they are very important not to neglect in your applications and are directly tied to the latest initiatives which will be seeking input of "actual or potential risk".

There are probably more of these than you think in your area, so look closely, and ask questions. Some of the other things that would be important to consider, although technically not considered "critical infrastructure" would be:

Public and Private schools and universities or colleges

☐ List total of students daily

## Hospitals

☐ List the number of beds
☐ What level of trauma center are they?

## Major manufacturing facilities

☐ Particularly if they use hazmats or are more than 100K sq. feet in size

## Trucking terminals for major trucking companies

Take a good drive through your primary response and mutual areas, make notes of these things and then call to get further information about them. This is all part of "risk assessment" which will be a critical part of successful grant applications now and in your future.

# 3. Step One: The Basics

*Proper Grant Strategy*

## Strategic Positioning

One of the very first things to do is take a good, hard look at your current or upcoming budget. Sometimes how you list line items in the budget can affect your ability to qualify for a particular grant. Many departments sabotage their own chances because they unintentionally place line items in their budgets, which would actually prohibit them from qualifying for certain funding opportunities in order to fund those items.

Tips

When you are looking at the budget, you need to take a close look at what "line" items you are listing and exactly how you are listing them. There is a clause attached to Federal and State grants that states that you cannot "supplant" funds.

The definition of Supplanting is:

☐ To deliberately reduce state or local funds because of the existence of grant funds

☐ To replace funding of a recipient's existing program with funds from a Federal grant. Federal grant statutes and regulations frequently prohibit this practice. Grants may also state that you cannot have a reduction in budget in prior or future years. Such as: "You would not qualify for staffing grants to hire one or more new personnel if your force has been reduced by more than 20% in the last few years."

This means, that if you have a line item in your budget for a vehicle and then you get a grant which gains you that vehicle, you will still have to buy the vehicle listed as a line item in your budget. You would not be able to transfer the money set aside in that line item to another line item and use it for something else. If you do that with a Federal grant, it would be fraud.

No No

In strategically looking at your budget, you should look at past grant programs and see what they have been traditionally funding over the past few years. If you see that there have been grants for "turnout gear", then do not put money in your budget and designate it for turnout gear. Put the money in the budget and call it "Personal Protective Equipment" or better yet just say "equipment." That definition of Personal Protective Equipment includes turnout gear, SCBAs ( self-contained breathing apparatus), flashlights, PASS alarms, and a few other items. That way if you do apply for the grant, and get an award for turnout gear, you will still be

Remember

www.HDGrants.com     33

Grant Writer's Handbook

able to use the money for some other piece of personal protective equipment such as SCBAs and would not be violating the supplanting rule.

While we are on the subject of strategically setting up your department, let us remember that you must set aside funding every year to be used as matching dollars for grants. We have seen many departments miss an excellent opportunity because they failed to have a line-item budget specifically for "grant matching funds."

No No

Contrary to popular myths usually perpetrated by a local board commissioner or citizen who is not current with current grant programs, most Federal/State grants are not totally free. They require a cash matching contribution, which is usually based upon the size of your budget or the population of the area you serve. This can range from 50% to as little as 5%, depending upon the program. Do not get caught unprepared. Set aside money in your budget each year so that you have funding available to apply for these grants and so if you are awarded, you can accept the grant.

Most funding sources frown highly on spending time and effort to read, analyze, and do the administrative paperwork associated with awarding a grant, only to have the intended recipient turn the grant down. This is a tremendous waste of time and effort for them and it raises red flags about your agency in applying for future grants. This is part of a comprehensive grant strategy in determining what will be required of you in the event of an award and checking to be sure that you can accept the award if chosen. It is very easy to go from being "a hero" of the agency for obtaining the grant, to being "a heel" because you failed to determine if the matching funds would be made available to accept the award.

Record keeping and statistical data are also big issues in strategic planning. Many departments will get into their grant narrative and realize that they cannot produce the data needed to support or justify the funding. Good, solid record keeping of everything that your department does, and keeping it constantly updated, will save you time and effort when facing a grant deadline. It is also essential in proving "need" for your agency.

Proving that there is "need" in a grant application is most often proved through the presentation of statistical data to support that contention. This is something that is very

## Step One: The Basics

critical to most grants. Maintaining proper reporting to your state and federal agencies is a necessity. Eligibility and award amounts are frequently set based upon "formulas." This is especially true in law enforcement grants where how much you are eligible to receive is determined by a formula used by computing your Uniform Crime Index numbers vs. your population. Other grants such as JAG (Justice Assistance Grant) require UCR ( Uniform Crime Report) reporting for at least three years before your agency can even apply.

Tracking your statistical data can go a long way in justifying "need" in a grant. Most reviewers will not consider your grant unless you provide statistical data to prove your problem. The old adage of " if it was not recorded it never occurred" is very much true in the world of grants. It is critical to keep accurate and up-to-date records to be able to prove that a problem exists. The job is not done till the paperwork is filed, and this is one of the reasons that you must file reports and keep accurate records.

---

Quoting national statistical data only goes part of the way in justifying need in a grant. If you cannot back that national data up with comparisons using local figures, your application will get rejected.

No No

---

### Forming A Grants Team

Getting properly prepared for a grant requires a lot of preparation. Departments that form grant teams consistently outperform those departments which do not. They get grants year after year, while you are still struggling to get your first one. Learn from their lessons! When using the team approach you should have one person that heads the team, compiles all the data and composes or writes the grant. This will insure that everyone does his or her part in a timely manner.

Remember the concept of T.E.A.M.

- ☐ **T**ogether
- ☐ **E**veryone
- ☐ **A**ccomplishes
- ☐ **M**ore

There are many things that have to be done in often in a very short period of time. Everyone has different levels of skill at certain tasks so choose the best person to perform particular tasks. You need to recruit interested, motivated people of many diverse skills to have a properly functioning grant team. The optimum number is usually 4-5 members who will accomplish much, much more in a shorter period, than one grant writer will.

Public Safety employees have little if any control of their actual time. Since responding to the calls for service is your first priority and responsibility, everything else becomes secondary to that. Grant deadlines are usually cast in stone and cannot be changed. The grant funding source does not care if you are answering a five alarm fire the day before the grant is due or that you have had a double homicide in town and you are working and cannot finish your grant on time. Utilizing a team concept mitigates this problem for you and in the event that you are called away, someone else can pick up the ball and carry it forward.

When looking for members for these teams you should look for:

☐ **Number Crunchers** - These are the people that know your budget and who understand and properly predict expenses that would be associated with many of these grant projects. You will also require their knowledge of the economic conditions of your area. One of the primary reasons that grants are rejected is providing an inadequate financial need statement and these individuals can home in on what is critical to your area.

They also are more cognizant of hidden charges or costs associated with running particular programs and can bring those issues to the forefront so that your application considers all angles involved in achieving a successful outcome.

As an example; if you were writing a grant program for "staffing needs" you may not know how much the city has to spend on providing uniforms, insurance, retirement, vacation, unemployment, and benefits for the position, yet these may be eligible costs under the grant award. If you did not include them in your application, then you would not be able to cover them with monies from your award.

The same can be said of making sure that you had extended warranty or service contracts (if allowed) on equipment that you were buying. If those costs are not included in the application, they will be ineligible expenses to be paid with your award money.

These persons are also responsible for seeing if the award would put you in a position where an OMBA-133 audit would be needed if you win the grant and it puts more than $500K in Federal funds in play in one fiscal year for your agency. They can figure the relative costs associated with conducting that audit. Since the grant requires this, it becomes an eligible expense as long as you account for it in the grant application. If you forget to include this in your application, there is no "do over" button to allow its addition and those cost would now have to be taken from your operational budget.

## Step One: The Basics

The OMB A-133 Memorandum can be seen in Appendix One at the end of this book. The full text can be read at http://www.whitehouse.gov/omb/circulars/a133/a133.pdf

☐ **Statisticians** - Who in your department can go through the records and dig out statistics for not only the department, but find the demographics regarding your population? This is information that must be included in every successful grant application, and assigning someone to this task should not be taken lightly. It requires an analytical mind to define and research the statistical information that might be relevant to your grant. The correct person will probably already have a strong working knowledge concerning your department's statistics and he or she should be familiar with where to go to retrieve such information.

A proper project description will include demographical information and statistical data to back up what you are claiming is wrong and how your department can mitigate that problem if granted funding. This information forms the basis of "need" and is a primary factor considered by reviewers when deciding who is, or is not, funded.

☐ **Computer Savvy Individuals** - They know how to navigate the web, change and store files, operate different programs and make spreadsheets etc. These are all tasks that are vital to a properly functioning grant team. The Internet has become your best asset in researching grant opportunities and in applying for them. However, it requires a good, solid computer background to efficiently and accurately find the information and then utilize it correctly. The advent of the GMS (Grant Management System) and the E-grants process by the U.S. government and most States has proven to be a real boon to departments that are isolated and with limited access to professionals or resources where this information is usually located.

This person can also prove critical to your application when Murphy's Law kicks in and your local ISP goes down or the computer locks up and loses your grant application data four hours before the deadline. Having someone who is prepared to deal with these "glitches" is essential.

When searching for this person look for the individual in your department who is always on the Internet or always comes to work with a laptop in their backpack. They will be the one that always choose their seat closest to the computer and are always ready to jump up and lend their "computer geekiness" to you when the computer freezes up or a hard drive crashes.

☐ **Out Of The Box Thinkers** - Grants exist primarily to develop new and better ways to do things. It is the "out-of-the-box thinkers" who come up with the ideas for programs such as, Community Oriented Policing or "RIT packs." They have an innate ability

www.HDGrants.com

to "visualize" how something should be done. They are a great asset to any team, especially when you have to come up with an idea that is innovative and original.

> **Remember**, it is the unique ideas that set your program apart from the others and often result in a successful grant application.

These are the people in your department that are always coming up with a better way to do something or saying" if we only had this we could do this". You know the type I am speaking of. That one person who always thinks there is a better way to do something or a faster way to do something. They are not always exactly right but you know what they say, "even a broken clock is correct twice a day".

Those person's brains are programmed to think differently from how many of us think. They have an innate ability to step away from the problem and view it in a different light. They see things from a perspective that we do not see but frequently lack the authority or initiative to implement or discuss what they see or even say something about it. This is someone you need on your team and they should encouraged to participate. Sometimes they are the ones who can actually form that nexus that must be created between your needs and the needs of the funding source.

- ☐ **Trainers** - Almost all grant programs have an element that requires training. It might be for the proper usage of a new piece of equipment, or a driver improvement program that is associated with a new piece of apparatus or any number of other things. The point is someone has to conduct the training, and if you do not include those costs associated with this training, you will be incurring additional costs that could have been covered in the grant award. Adding these people to your team will ensure that your grant application is properly developed and takes these hidden costs and time constraints into consideration. This allows you to present a more comprehensive plan to the funding source for consideration.

- ☐ **Upper Management** - We all have bosses that we have to answer to; whether that be the Chief of the Department, City Manager or the governing board of elected officials. Remember it is the head of the agency that has to sign off on these grants so, keeping them informed is essential to the grant process. These people control the purse strings. Management has to sign off on the "assurances" that accompany all grant applications and they also have to make the decisions that can affect your program such as:

## Step One: The Basics

- ☐ Do we have the required cash match?
- ☐ Can we keep up with the reporting requirements?
- ☐ Will we be able to maintain this level of budget and satisfy the terms of the grant award?
- ☐ Are we going to be able to absorb the cost of the new person within the required time frame or maintain the maintenance cost?
- ☐ Is this the ONLY application being filed for this program (especially important in large metropolitan areas with different precincts or station houses)?

Checklist

If you don't include these people in the development process from the very start, you could wind up like one major city recently did.

### Case Study:

This particular city's fire department worked with us for over a month developing a very comprehensive application, asking for a new fireboat because they had been given fire suppression responsibilities for a major U.S. port. The Lieutenant assigned to do the grant, worked diligently on developing a winning application for approximately $75,000.00. On the morning, that this application was due, there was a desperate email message from this Lieutenant. When we contacted him, he related that his application was refused online; because the US Fire Administration had another application from their agency, (a Captain at another station had submitted a grant application for something else). So, the Lieutenant had wasted a month because he had not cleared his application process. Not only was the fireboat application never submitted but the application the other station house submitted was rejected.

### Lesson Learned:

Be sure the left hand knows what the right had is doing.

Remember

I have had many great applications developed by grant writers, who we have personally trained, and they have developed a fine application which was comprehensive in scope except they forgot to check with the Chief of the agency and address their concerns before developing the application. In the 11th hour of submitting the grant it was presented to the Chief and he wanted "flashlights" in this grant. The writer had not included them because he knew they were a lower priority than the other items being requested on your grant and that they would score low, bringing the overall score of the grant down. Resultantly the Chief added this $1000 dollars for flashlights to the grant application, unbeknownst to the original

www.HDGrants.com

Grant Writer's Handbook

grant writer. It was not until the grant was later rejected that the grant writer learned that the Chief had added the flashlights to the grant application.

This act, done without consideration of other known factors, caused a loss of $189K in new SCBA equipment for this department. Blame here is equally shared between the two. The grant writer should have recognized and involved the Chief of the Department in his initial planning stages of the grant and the Chief should have recognized that the grant writer knows the grant program and had done his job properly. If the two had simply talked first, the grant would have been funded and the Chief would have been sent directed to apply to a local corporate funding course for those flashlights.

> ☐ **Stakeholders** - Stakeholders are private and public organizations, or groups of people (senior citizens, homeowners, merchants, non-profit organizations etc.) that will be impacted should your application be accepted or denied.

You should identify as many stakeholders as possible for the problem you select. Each stakeholder may bring different knowledge and leverage for impacting the problem. The more stakeholders that are identified, the more resources you will have to throw at the problem.

Some communities have found that the problem-solving effort progresses most efficiently if only two or three stakeholders — a core group — work on the problem throughout the project. Other, more peripheral stakeholders, often have something to contribute at specific stages of the project, but not throughout the entire effort.

For instance, here's a sample problem and a list of potential stakeholders and partners.

A mid-sized eastern city of 35,000, with a relatively low crime rate, had experienced a series of fast food delivery robberies. On average, there was one robbery per month, and a number of fast-food stores refused to deliver to a mostly low-income, predominantly black neighborhood where many of the robberies were taking place. A resident of the neighborhood effectively complained about the lack of delivery service, and started a petition to change the policy. The city council began considering a proposal to require delivery to all residents, regardless of their location.

Based upon the above, the following groups were identified as "Stakeholders" for this project:

Checklist
☐ Law enforcement
☐ Customers in "no delivery" neighborhood
☐ Fast food delivery people

40  www.HDGrants.com

## Step One: The Basics

- ☐ Fast food management
- ☐ National fast food delivery chains
- ☐ National Restaurant Association
- ☐ Local NAACP chapter
- ☐ Local legislators
- ☐ Local media

You will save your department and management a lot of headaches and complaints by including these people in the planning of your project and seeking their input. People that have a hand in developing the program are much more likely to cooperate with your efforts to run a successful grant program and are much less likely to end up filing a complaint with your city council or the media. When you include them in the process from the beginning, this is far less likely to occur.

Those organizations which have a grants team in place will find that the grants process is much easier to manage and manipulate the process.

## *DUNS (DUNS Universal Numbering System) Number*

One of the problems that faced the Federal Grants System was keeping track of taxpayer's money.

Traditional auditing systems were inaccurate and with so many federal agencies, the money was simply not being tracked. It was also determined that many recipients of grant funds were receiving additional grant monies that duplicated assistance already received. Many had never been audited to see if the money was being used in the manner specified.

They learned as well, that many of the Federal granting agencies had no idea what other grant monies had been received or were under consideration. In not knowing how much was being held by some of these recipients, it led to the feeling that many eligible grant recipients were being ignored at the expense of other more fortunate grantees. This led to a media blitz charging the U.S. government with not showing proper stewardship of tax monies.

A system had to be devised that would allow all agencies in the Federal government to keep track of the distributions – who had received what grants and what the status of those grants were. It was also indirectly responsible for the governments shift in what is currently known as "performance grants" and the initiative being undertaken to form the E-grants process. This move resulted in the formation of the Grants Management System or GMS, which is the system used by most Federal grant agencies today.

www.HDGrants.com

Grant Writer's Handbook

In developing this electronic grants application system, a method was needed to identify exactly who each recipient or applicant was. It would also facilitate the "tracking" of each of the grant funds given to these recipients, where Federal money was being distributed, and its utilization.

Eventually the Federal Government turned to corporate America for solutions. Much as a social security number identifies an individual citizen in this country; a system was needed which would positively identify each grant recipient. It was initially suggested that the Federal Employee Identification Number (FEIN) would serve to accomplish this task. However, there was a problem with that system as well; agencies within agencies used that number (fire and police departments used the same number). There had to be another solution, and there was.

It came from Dun & Bradstreet. For years, they had been the leading authority in tracking the business interests and company information for private corporations across the U.S. They already had a system in place that identified each of these individual entities.

> **Must Do** — From that system, the Duns Universal Numbering System (DUNS) was born and is now a requirement of every agency applying for Federal funding. Since 2003, the Federal Government has required all applicants and recipients of Federal funding to have a DUNS number.

If your agency has been the recipient or has applied through the GMS for a grant since 2003, you should already have a DUNS number assigned. If you have never applied, you will need to contact them and have a number assigned to your agency.

The DUNS number is a unique nine-character identification number provided, at no charge, by the commercial company Dun & Bradstreet.

To apply for the DUNS number, call 866-705-5711 or apply online at http://fedgov.dnb.com/webform .

If you call the process takes about ten minutes. Be prepared to answer the following questions:

**Checklist**
- a) Name of business
- b) Business address
- c) Local phone number
- d) Name of the CEO/business owner
- e) Legal structure of the business (corporation, partnership, proprietorship)
- f) Year business started

## Step One: The Basics

- g) Primary line of business
- h) Total number of employees (full and part time)

You also may obtain a DUNS number on-line at the D&B website (www.dnb.com ), which may take up to 14 business days.

### The Central Contractor Registry (CCR)

The DUNS number is also a prerequisite for another applicant organizational requirement: registration in the Federal Government's Central Contractor Registry (http://www.ccr.gov/ ). Registration in this system (CCR) is a requirement for all grantees and a current requirement for grantees applying for federal assistance through Grants.gov (http://www.grants.gov/).

Many properly ask us why they need this number since they are not a contractor. Well, the simple truth is, that if you accept a grant award of Federal funding you are in fact forming a contract with the Federal government to perform certain deeds or services in exchange for that funding. Hence the requirement to be registered with the CCR. Keep in mind that you will have to renew this number every few years as well.

The revised SF 424, Application for Federal Assistance, which includes the DUNS number field is available on the Office of Management and Budget's website at http://www.whitehouse.gov/omb/grants/grants_forms.html .

### NIMS (National Incident Management System) Compliance

On February 28, 2003, President Bush issued Homeland Security Directive-5 (HSPD-5) which directed the Department of Homeland Security Director to develop and administer a National Incident Management System (NIMS). To be eligible for DHS grants, you must participate in NIMS. This is one of your first steps that must be undertaken if you expect to benefit from the grants available at DHS.

Must Do

### Mandatory Participation for Grant Eligibility

Part of the directive's language states that "Federal departments and agencies make the adoption of NIMS by State and Local organizations a condition in order to participate in Federal preparedness programs by FY05". In other words, you must now be compliant with all current NIMS mandates to be eligible to apply for DHS grants after Oct. 1, 2004.

As further guidance, the NIMS Integration Center (NIC) encourages all emergency personnel with a direct role in emergency preparedness, incident management, or response to

www.HDGrants.com

## Grant Writer's Handbook

take the NIMS courses. Many are offered free-of-charge through the Emergency Management Institute at: http://training.fema.gov/IS/.

### What Does That Mean?

If your department does not comply with the NIMS mandates, you will not be eligible to participate in their funding streams. This requirement applies to everyone involved in public safety: law enforcement, EMS, rescue services, local governments, emergency management, etc.

NIMS is a comprehensive, national approach to incident management that is applicable to all jurisdictional levels, across all functional disciplines. The whole intent of the NIMS program is two-fold:

- ☐ Be applicable across a full spectrum of potential incidents and hazard scenarios, regardless of size or complexity.
- ☐ Improve coordination and cooperation between public and private entities in a variety of domestic incident management activities.

To view NIMS Compliance Objectives for States, Territories, Tribal Nations, and Local Governments go to the NIMS Integration Center (NIC) Website at http://www.fema.gov/emergency/nims/

Since NIMS compliance is such an integral part of the funding process for DHS it is highly suggested that you make NIMS compliance within your agency a mandatory compliance factor for your personnel.

**Must Do:** The statute states that you must be in compliance with all CURRENT mandates and as such you need to be constantly vigilant for changes or new requirements being promulgated. While on the site listed above it is highly suggested that you sign up for their "list serve" of NIMS alerts and you will automatically receive alerts and updates on staying compliant with NIMS mandates and objectives. NIMS compliance is a key part of applying for any DHS funding.

Since this is not a course on NIMS it is up to you to check the web sites provided and insure that you and your agency is compliant. It is our understanding that Regional NIMS compliance officers are being assigned throughout the country that will have responsibility for ensuring compliance by grantees.

**Remember:** Remember in order to receive Federal funding your agency must be NIMS compliant. In years past DHS has been taking a "soft compliance" outlook in regards to compliance with NIMS. That is no longer the case. They are now tracking compliance with a tool called NIMSCAST and have indicated that NIMS compliance will be

## Step One: The Basics

checked and confirmed. Do not ignore this requirement as it could very well result in you being denied an award if during technical review of your grant it was discovered that your agency is not in compliance.

### Checklist For Establishing Grant Strategy Within A Public Safety Agency.

- ☐ Find and properly train the right person to lead the agencies grant efforts
- ☐ Analyze the current ops budget for areas frequently funded grants
- ☐ Set aside matching dollar funds
- ☐ Keep accurate and up-to-date records and statistics
- ☐ Keep all required state and national reporting requirements up to date
- ☐ Form a grants team within the agency using those person's specific skill sets
- ☐ Obtain or ascertain your DUNS number
- ☐ Obtain or register with the Central Contactor Registry
- ☐ Be certain your agency is in full current compliance with NIMS mandates

Checklist

## Finding Funding

### Website Resources

Actually locating a funding source can be a daunting and often times frustrating task. It is really not just as simple as Googling "grants for a squad car". Typically those requests could result in literally thousands of returns to read it and the time that takes to read and digest that data can be a huge obstacle for you to overcome. More likely the returns you will get are articles from agencies that got a squad car and not grants. There are methods for speeding up this process which this chapter will discuss.

Finding funding takes patience, time and the ability to read comprehensively. You will have to read a lot, as there is simply no way to go about it in any other way. Nobody has yet to develop a computer program that you can simply type in "find me a grant for purchasing widgets" and an application appears before your eyes. Believe me when I say if it was out there we would be the first to buy or subscribe to it. However, with practice, most aspiring grant writers can find some tools that will aid in this search and discovering exactly where and what to look for in these areas can make the quest more manageable and less of a burden for you.

Tips

The best tool available to you right now is the Internet. A few mouse clicks here or there, signing up for some automated services that deliver grant information directly to you and just good old plain reading will result in success at locating funding sources. You should also not discount the Return on Investment of having professional grant consultants who you can

www.HDGrants.com                                                                                                       45

call upon to steer you to opportunities that they are familiar with. The return on investment dollars with them can quite quickly amount to a 100:1 ROI.

Below you will find a partial list of the web sites that we frequently use to find grants and to research data. There is also a brief description of what you will find there and how best to use it. You will find all of these sites helpful, and if you look hard enough, you may find some funding that your agency could qualify for and will fit your needs.

### Federal Register (Daily email with TOC)

http://listserv.access.gpo.gov

The Federal Register could be best described as the daily newspaper of the Federal Government. Anything that happens of consequence in the Federal Government is usually published in the Federal Register. This can include information about new grant programs being announced, changes to grant programs, new levels of funding being set, new grant programs being formed, and modifications to various programs.

The Daily Table of Contents (TOC) is a list serve that you can sign up for which daily will deliver the TOC to your email box. This daily document can lead you to information that gives you a decided advantage over others in terms of timely notification. It lists each department of the Federal Government where a significant event has occurred, They list meetings that are going to take place, Presidential Disaster declarations, changes in statutes and or compliance issues and they also list information about various grant programs from FEMA, DHS, DOI and other agencies within the government.

This is one of those things that arrive in your mailbox and you need to take a minute or so of your time daily to scan. Remember it is a TOC, not the actual information. When you do see something with a keyword in it like "grant program modification" or "grant announcement" you should stop and click the provided link and read the details.

We frequently find advance notice or actual announcements about grant programs here first. Do not be afraid to investigate an item listed here that, on the surface, might not seem to be relevant to you. Many of the programs we discover here are obscure and require reading deeper into the documents to find relevancy.

As an example; I have found opportunities for EMS and rescue squads by looking at announcements of grant programs from the Center for Disease Control or from the Health and Rural Services Administration that have led to agencies receiving a new ambulance or cardiac monitors.

## Step One: The Basics

I once found a 5 year program to hire and run a Fire Prevention Education program with $100K per year being provided to a fire department and it was from the CDC. We have found community siren systems from National Oceanographic and Atmospheric Administration.

You have to learn to read comprehensively and keep an open mind when perusing these sites. The benefits can be great if you choose to do so.

### Federal Funds Express

http://www.house.gov/ffr/resources_all.shtml.

The Federal Funds Express is a clearinghouse for grant related information for the Federal Government. It operates as a portal to other government maintained websites that contain grant information.

### Grants.gov

www.grants.gov/

This site is one of the sites you will visit frequently if you become involved in the world of grants. It was developed to be the electronic portal entry site for entities wanting to apply to Federal Grant programs. It was developed in part as a response to the Federal Paperwork Reduction Act.

In the near future it will be impossible to file a grant application to the Federal Government on paper. The sheer volume of applicants to Federal programs is staggering and continually growing. As the economy falters further, the number of applicants seeking help from the Federal government grows exponentially every year. Storing and processing paper applications generates a storage, filing and logistical problem of immense proportions for Washington DC. As a result, they simply cannot deal with the paperwork generated. It is also a much "greener" solution to handle these matters electronically.

---

Grants.gov offers a partial solution to these issues. On many grant programs you have to use the grants.gov portal in order to access the information about the program and to actually apply. As such it will require you to register and set up a user account. This can take several weeks to accomplish while awaiting a user ID and password, so it is not something that you should wait to do; get it done now so that you are not hindered in applying at a later time when a deadline may be looming. Part of the process of registering with grants.gov will include providing your DUNS and CCR numbers.   **Must Do !**

---

Grants.gov provides a pretty easy search engine to use in looking for funding opportunities. However, as of this writing, it still leaves much to be desired.

Grant Writer's Handbook

We have found its most useful function, in addition to being the point of entry to apply for these opportunities, is the ability to set alerts for you. If you are browsing this website and see a program which interests you, it is relatively easy to set an alert for yourself. When the program opens for applications or anything of significance happens that might affect this program, you will receive notification through your email. You may also request email notices of all grant notices once a day as well as notices for specific categories or agencies.

### CFDA (Catalog of Federal Domestic Assistance)

http://www.cfda.gov/

The CFDA is the "Bible" for grant seekers from the Feds. As its name infers, if the Federal government has a program which provides any domestic assistance in any form to our citizens, then it is listed in the CFDA.

This could be housing and rent assistance, food stamp programs, and of course grants. If you have ever looked at a Federal grant program announcement you will always see a CFDA # listed for it.

This site has tremendous search engine capability. You can search for funding opportunities by type of assistance, agency sponsoring the program or category of assistance being sought. The possibilities are endless here. It also has the ability to perform Boolean searches on keywords.

Once you have selected a program which you have interest in the CFDA will display a document which is packed full of relevant information which can save you a whole lot of time in searching for funding opportunities. See Appendix Two for more information.

If you refer to the example Assistance to Firefighters Grant announcement online (http://hdgrants.com/Grant-Writers-Handbook.asp) you will see what one of these notices looks like. From this notice you can discern a number of things very quickly.

The first thing to look for is under the header title of "Applicant Eligibility". This section tells you who is eligible to apply to this program. As an individual agency you need to be looking for the words, "State, and local government agencies of the US and its territories". Be cautious here and read closely if you see it stating that "only States" or SAA (State Administering Agent) may apply because you, as an individual agency of a local government, would be excluded and that would mean that application to that program will probably be through a process run through your individual state.

## Step One: The Basics

The next most critical thing to look for is if there is going to be funding available in this particular year. For that information you should look for the header titled "Financial Information" on this form. There will be a subsection header under this section that reads "Obligations". You will see a year and an amount listed such as FY2010 $550,000,000. If you do not see an obligation listed for the current year, the chances are the program did not receive funding for that year or has been abandoned.

Next you should look for the "Objectives" and "Uses and use restrictions" portions of this document. If you see that what you are looking for is eligible, bingo, you are in the game. If on the contrary you see that what you are trying to do is listed as ineligible, then you can stop reading the notice at this point and move on to something else.

Other items of interest on this CFDA document that you will find helpful would include:

- ☐ Application Award Process
- ☐ Deadlines
- ☐ Contact Information
- ☐ Formula and Matching Requirements
- ☐ Post Assistance Requirements

Checklist

## Examples of Funded Projects

### Responders Knowledge Base (RKB)

https://www.rkb.us/

This site provides a listing of available grants with a link to the Approved Equipment List (AEL). This information will prove extremely valuable since most of the equipment that you will request on grant will have to be on the AEL.

### FundsNet

www.fundsnetservices.com

Another clearinghouse of grant information by type of assistance being sought.

BJA Bureau of Justice Assistance

http://www.ojp.usdoj.gov/BJA/funding/current-opp.html

www.HDGrants.com

# Grant Writer's Handbook

COPS (Community Oriented Policing Services)

http://www.cops.usdoj.gov/Default.asp?Item=46

Listing of current funding opportunities offered by Community Oriented Policing Services such as Tribal Resources Grant Program, COPS Recovery Hiring Program, Save Our Schools Program etc.

## OJJDP (Office of Juvenile Justice and Delinquency Prevention)

http://ojjdp.ncjrs.org/

Under the leadership of its Administrator and through its components, OJJDP sponsors research, program, and training initiatives; develops priorities and goals and sets policies to guide federal juvenile justice issues; disseminates information about juvenile justice issues; and awards funds to states to support local programming.

## ONDCP (Office on Nat'l Drug Control Policy)

http://www.whitehousedrugpolicy.gov/

The principal purpose of ONDCP is to establish policies, priorities, and objectives for the Nation's drug control program. The goals of the program are to reduce illicit drug use, manufacturing, and trafficking, drug-related crime and violence, and drug-related health consequences.

## JUSTNET NIJ

http://www.ojp.usdoj.gov/nij/funding/current.htm

OJP (Office of Justice Programs)

http://www.ojp.usdoj.gov/

## OJP, by State

http://www.ojp.usdoj.gov/saa/index.htm

This site will be very useful in finding funding available through your SAA such as JAG, Paul Coverdell Forensic Science Improvement Program, Violence Against Women and many others.

## DHS (Department of Homeland Security)

www.dhs.gov

## Step One: The Basics

The DHS website is huge, growing and changing on an almost daily basis. It is a plethora of information concerning anything having to do with DHS or any office under the umbrella of DHS. Numerous links and great resources are available here for those who browse and dig through it. Not only grant opportunities listed here but also lots of free information and training available that you may never have heard about. It is also good to watch their press releases column as well because they frequently refer to projected funding levels and/or changes proposed for various grant programs.

### FEMA/US Fire Administration

http://www.usfa.dhs.gov/fireservice/index.shtm

This is a primary website if you are Fire /EMS/Rescue or Emergency Management. Not only a resource for funding opportunities about Fire Act Grants but also a great place to gather National statistical information and reports about fires in general for supportive documentation in grant applications to their programs.

### NIST (National Inst. of Standards & Technology)

www.csrc.nist.gov/grants

Primary area of focus for this organization is in IT Security concerns as they relate to critical infrastructure. They sometimes have R&D development grants for those purposes especially as it relates to new or emerging technology in those areas.

### Federal Agencies & Commissions

www.whitehouse.gov/government/independent-agencies.html

This is a website run by the White House which is a reference source for you to find out "who is in charge of what" in the US Government.

### OMB (Ofc of Management & Budgets)

www.whitehouse.gov/omb/grants

Without exception all Federal grants have rules and regulations controlling aspects of application, audits, reporting requirements, procurement etc which are promulgated through the Office of Management & Budget ( OMB). Many of these rules and regulations are referred to within RFPs for grants as "circulars". This is a link to the website where those circulars and other information that concerns management aspects of the grants resides at.

www.HDGrants.com

Grant Writer's Handbook

### State & Local Govt. on the Net

www.statelocalgov.net/index.cfm

A directory of state and local government agencies across the Nation

### Information Technology Initiatives

www.it.ojp.gov/index.jsp

Office of Justice Programs website which deals with initiatives involving information sharing technologies amongst criminal justice agencies.

### Grants Net, Health & Human Svcs

www.hhs.gov/grantsnet

HHS awards grants for more than 300 programs and is the largest grant-awarding agency in the Federal government. It is not unusual to find opportunities from within this agency that require partnerships with first responder agencies for drug and substance abuse, mental health issues etc. It usually takes some digging to ferret these opportunities out but they can be quite beneficial and offer an alternative funding resource.

### Public Safety Foundation of America

www.psfa.us

The PSFA funds new or ongoing projects for the betterment of the public safety communications community. Eligible projects include:

- ☐ Planning and Coordination – expenses related to determining how best to plan for or coordinate a major organizational public safety communications project.
- ☐ Strategic Initiatives – expenses related to high level programs addressing organizational challenges and issues related to improving the overall quality of a public safety communications agency or organization.
- ☐ PSAP Equipment and Technology – expenses associated with the physical equipment required for an acquisition or upgrade within a public safety communications agency or organization.
- ☐ Education – expenses associated with developing and implementing programs to educate public safety agencies and other stakeholders about the importance of public safety communications or public safety communications issues.

## Step One: The Basics

### FedWorld

www.fedworld.gov

The FedWorld.gov web site is a gateway to government information. This site is managed by the National Technical Information Service (NTIS) as part of its information management mandate.

### First Gov

www.firstgov.gov

Another electronic portal for accessing information about just about any aspect of Federal government including grant information and information about specific agencies and their functions.

### MetaSoft

http://foundationsearch.com/

This is a paid service costing approx. $3K per year to be a member. It offers probably the single most comprehensive website in the world concerning private foundations and corporate grant making organizations and individuals. The website can tell you such information as how much money was given in your area and by whom and for what purposes. It employs a huge number of foreign employees who glean information daily from all newspapers in the US and also tracks IRS forms required to be filed by Charitable Giving organizations. This allows the user to perform very targeted searches for grant funding opportunities with a more specific and direct approach. It is rather pricey at first glance however; the information leads to far more successful fund raising efforts than anything else offered when searching for non-Federal or State funded grant opportunities.

### Foundation Center

http://foundationcenter.org/

Another paid service provided here in the U.S. for approx. $2K per year covers private foundation and corporate charitable giving. They track IRS forms and maintain a database of information gleaned from those forms in order to perform targeted searches for funding sources amongst corporate and private foundations.

### eCivis

http://ecivis.com/

Grant Writer's Handbook

A paid grant information provider service with good customer service and offering a wide variety of services, relevant data sources that are kept current and represent good value to the municipal and local government organizations.

## The Politics Of Grants

Tips

Obtaining funding many times is about building relationships. Get to know the program managers of the state programs you will be applying for, these relationships will go a long way in helping you get funding. Foundations work the same way, get to know people on the board of Foundations in your area. These acquaintances could gain you an invitation to apply for funding, even if the Foundation does not normally fund public safety agencies.

The Federal grant system is at times a political football game and anyone not willing to admit that politics plays a role in the game is only fooling themselves. Remember, grant money comes from Federal taxes and is used to pave roads, develop housing, build schools, fund social and health programs, and fund public safety programs.

Every US Congressional Representative maintains an office in Washington, DC, and usually a local office in their home district. There is usually a staff member that has a role as the grants liaison person. They are the direct line to that representative. It is their job to make sure that, as a constituent, your opinions, concerns, and needs are addressed. It is their job to assist you in accessing and applying for Federal grant assistance.

Whenever you apply for a grant, it is a good idea to keep the local US Congressional and State representatives and their staff members informed of this fact. These are all people you should make a point of knowing and advising about your departmental needs. It is a "Best Practice" to send a copy of your completed grant application to them with a cover letter asking for a letter of support to be submitted with your grant application. Always be sure to include in that letter the application number assigned to your grant (if using an E-grant process) and the proper address to submit the letter. The RFP or program guidance will usually relate the proper procedure and where to have these letters of support sent.

Always respectfully ask for them to assist your department's application in any way that they can. Many grant programs give additional consideration to applications with letters of support from elected officials; other programs will allow you to send letters of support with your application. These letters can go a long way in moving your application to the top of the funding pile.

Remember, these are elected officials and receiving the funds for a new fire truck or communication center in your town means happy voters on Election Day. At the same time,

54                                                                                            www.HDGrants.com

## Step One: The Basics

you need to remember that if they do not know you are seeking Federal assistance, they can't help you.

It is all about networking. Get to know the grant staff person of both your US Congressional, and State Legislators, on a first name basis. This person can be, literally, a lifeline. A vital link in your grant chain, they can also be an extremely valuable resource for finding other grant programs at the State and Local levels. It can really pay off big for you to be on their mailing lists so that you are notified whenever there is money available.

It is also a good idea to let them know what projects you are trying to accomplish. Many opportunities exist and pass their desks daily. If they know you have a project pending and see an opportunity, they will call you regarding information about how to take advantage of it.

Additionally, a number of State Legislative representatives in some states - PA and NY come to mind - have what is known as "member items" money. This is discretionary money they may allocate within their respective districts for various projects to benefit their constituency.

Congressional intervention can also make the difference when you have been rejected for a grant and you absolutely, positively have to have this project funded. Having an established, ongoing relationship with your local Congressional and State representatives can get your project placed into a Congressional Earmark category, which could mean a nice check to your agency for that project.

These are the "pork" projects that we mentioned earlier, like the "$150,000 to study "cow chips" as a fuel alternative" or the $1.5 million dollar new school which just happens to be named after the US Senator who gets that district the money to build it. We may or may not agree with the practice, but it occurs every day in Washington, DC and you might eventually be faced with no alternative other than to turn to a congressional earmark for funding.

Political savvy is also necessary at the State and Local levels, as well. If you have ever been to your State Administering Agency website, you will see that a number of Federal grant programs are strictly controlled through that agency. Each of these programs will have a program contact. Having a networking relationship with these individuals is a good practice, as they can assist you in getting your project funded.

Know who these people are and make sure they know you. Call them frequently, exchange e-mails regularly and let them know of the problems you are trying to resolve. You never know when you may get a call from that person telling you about a pool of money that

would be just perfect for your project. Take assertive steps to assure that you are within their networking rings. It is well worth the effort.

One of our seminar students took this information to heart and upon returning to his hometown, picked up the phone and established contact with the grants person in his local Congressman's office. This initial phone conversation resulted in him receiving not one, but three phone calls within the next month from that grants staff person. Consequently, his agency benefited to the tune of over $50,000. To this day he averages better than $5K per year coming in funding from information supplied to him from that grants liaison staff person.

Finding out who your Congressional Representatives are and what committees they serve on is not difficult to do. Information such as this is easily located through a search on the Internet. A good place to start is the Congressional Directory, which can be accessed at www.gpoaccess.gov/cdirectory/index.html. Another great source is the blue pages in your local phone book.

# 4. Step Two: You Found A Grant

*Reviewing Request For Proposal (Rfp)/Guidelines*

---
Key Point # 1 – If you take away all the reasons that a reviewer has to deny your application; they are usually left with no choice but to fund your grant!

Must Do

---

    The RFP or Program Guidance gives you information critical to assuring that you do not give them a reason to deny your application. It is the rulebook for the grant game. Remember; it is their money and if you want their money, you have to play by their rules. Follow those rules to the letter and you get funded.

    This section will guide you through understanding and comprehending the Request for Proposal (RFP) or grant application guidelines. The RFP is your outline to the requirements for your proposal. You can think about this as the "rule" book for this particular grant. Examining, reading and re-reading this document several times allows you to develop an outline documenting the critical information in this document. Up to 50% of grant proposals fail because the writer did not follow the RFP requirements or missed some critical element that was in the RFP.

    You should always begin by reading the RFP carefully. This allows the reader to get a sense of what the grant program is about. It also establishes whether to continue reading deeper into the document or to continue the application process.

    On the subsequent second and third readings, you should have several highlighters. Typically we will use "green" to mark things that are considered "eligibility issues," "red" to denote items that are "ineligible" or would actually "hurt your application" and "blue" to highlight "program priorities," or items that are "critical to the applications success or would gain you higher considerations or higher scoring".

---
You should use color highlighters when doing this and this is why. The human mind, unless you are one of the unfortunate 8% of the population who are color blind, is pre-programmed to view color and place special significance to it. That is why in nature the males of species are brightly colored or poisonous plants are red. Think about it, do you like to watch black and white TV or color? We as humans react and interpret things differently when they are colored.

Tips

---

www.HDGrants.com        57

# Grant Writer's Handbook

Red typically signifies stop or danger. Green is used or interpreted to mean "go" or that something is "good". You can better prepare yourself to comprehensively read and understand something better, if you use color.

When you read the RFP the second time, keep those highlighters handy, and mark good things or eligible things in the RFP using the green highlighter. When you see things that will be prohibited or that are ineligible or would cause a "red flag" to be raised with a reviewer, use the red highlighter. If you see things that will gain you extra points or additional/higher consideration, mark them in blue. After you have done this to the whole document, now go back and re-read it again. You will be surprised to find how much these colors help you to notice things more quickly and place the proper significance with what they are saying.

## What Should I Be Looking For?

### 1. Is my organization eligible to apply?

There are often requirements that you must be a nonprofit or have "501c(3) IRS status, as is the case with many private and corporate foundation grants.

- ☐ Some grants only allow the State to apply or the SAA. You should check to be sure that a local unit of government can apply to the grant or program you are reviewing.
- ☐ Sometimes you will need to be associated with or servicing certain ethnic groups.
- ☐ There may also be requirements for being located in specific geographical or economic areas.
- ☐ There could be a list or link attached to the RFP listing the agencies that are eligible. This would be common on formula grants.
- ☐ You may have to be serving a community of underserved or economically disadvantaged persons.
- ☐ You might need to have a rural designation or a certain level of population.

**Tips**

If you have a question about your agencies eligibility, you should always call the program contact. It is better to find out, before you begin, to avoid wasting time preparing a grant application only to find that you were ineligible.

### 2. What are the restrictions?

- ☐ Restrictions may be in place which prohibit you from applying if you are a Federal agency or if you have certain responsibilities that involve Federal lands

## Step Two: You Found A Grant

- ☐ You may have to be providing services to typically underserved or ethnic groups in order to apply.
- ☐ You may also have to collaborate with certain other groups in the community in order to apply.
- ☐ Certain types of equipment or programs may be ineligible for this grant
- ☐ It is not unusual to see equipment restrictions for vehicles, real estate, weapons, yachts, and tanks .
- ☐ You may also have to determine if the equipment you are wanting to buy is listed on a Standardized Equipment List (SEL) or Authorized Equipment List (AEL) when using grants for DHS programs. This list is maintained by the Responder Knowledge Base (RKB) and can be accessed at www.rkb.us/. The Responders Knowledge Base will also provide links to grants with the equipment available or allowed from the AEL listed for that grant.
- ☐ What activities are allowed and what are the restrictions
- ☐ Check these areas carefully. If you have hiring a new employees included in your program, check to be sure you can use this funding for hiring.
- ☐ This area may also limit you in what percentage of costs are allowable for things like administration or training and travel.

### How many grants will be awarded?

- ☐ Look at how many awards will be made and then think about how many agencies, like yours, are likely to apply. If there are only going to be 10 grants given out for $250,000.00, your chances of getting that grant, are greatly reduced. You need to weigh the chances, against the result.

---

We always encourage you to apply for as many grant programs as you possibly can, however, common sense must prevail. Do not waste time on grant programs where you have very little chance of success.

**Tips**

---

Consider the size of your agency and your problems compared to a larger agency. Then check the RFP's goals and priorities. You can usually determine if this RFP is targeting larger agencies and if you would have a chance of being awarded.

### What is the average monetary size of the grant?

- ☐ What is the highest and lowest amount to be awarded?

Looking back at past lists of awards for certain programs can also show you what the average award is likely to be or by seeing how many applied, you can figure that average award

### Grant Writer's Handbook

for the funding available in the current program. Grants are a game of odds and playing the odds results in more funding success. Stick within the averages for best results.

- ☐ Determine the average size of most grants by dividing the total dollar amount to be awarded by the number of grants to be awarded. In most cases, it is better to shoot for the average as opposed to requesting the maximum amount.
- ☐ Will the award be large enough to fulfill your needs? Paying close attention to this area will help you to determine what a reasonable request should look like.

Grants are a numbers game and grant makers usually try to fund as many different agencies as they possibly can. This is also why most DHS grants will require you to talk about "cost benefit" in your application narrative.

Requesting a reasonable amount of money keeps the grant reviewer from running up the "greedy flag" —a position you do not want to see your application in. The fact that there is a maximum award should not be the reason that you request the full amount.

Tips

Key Point #2 -Successful grant writers should add three small words to their thought process when developing any grant application: NEEDY, NOT GREEDY! Do not ask for a Cadillac, if a VW will do the job!

*Is my department willing and able to comply with the rules of the RFP?*

- ☐ There are usually interim reports and a final report required. These may also include financial reports as well. Make sure that the person who is responsible for these reports will be able to complete them and file them on schedule. Failure to complete and file reports can result in rescinding the funding or preventing your agency from applying for future grants until this reporting is up to date.
- ☐ Will you have to do an evaluation of the programs impact or effectiveness?
  - Evaluations are a part of many grant programs.
  - Some of these can be self-evaluations, while others will require that a third party agency conduct the evaluation and report the results.
  - Does you city or agency have the needed resources to meet the matching dollar requirements?
  - This is one of the first things you should determine. We have seen many ambitious young grant writers develop a great program, only to take the final application to the City Manager or Chief and have him say "we don't have the matching dollars to do this."

## Step Two: You Found A Grant

Be sure to check when the matching funds must be paid and from where those funds can originate. You generally cannot use leftover funding from a previous grant to pay cash matching requirements in a new grant. It is not uncommon to see language that states the matching funds may be paid at any time within the performance period. Depending upon the review and award process you may find that as many as two of your departments FY budget cycles may pass before you would have to pay the matching funds.

**Must Do**

You should also keep in mind that once you have a grant award letter in your hand from the Federal Government stating it is paying 80-90% of an items cost, a commercial lending institution would consider that as equity and you would be a good credit risk for a long term low interest loan to cover the matching funds and be able to accept the grant award.

### What is the grant projected period?

- ☐ Most Federal grant programs give you 12 months from date of award to complete your grant program, but longer periods are common as well. Most hiring initiative programs, such as the Universal Hiring Program (UHP) for the DOJ (under the COPS program) or the SAFER Fire Act grant, are 2-4 year programs. Many of the multiple year projects will require you to reapply each year for continuation funding. Once again if you are not up to date on reports or have failed to comply with the grant in any way you may not get the continuation funding.

### Who is the contact and how do I reach them?

- ☐ There are usually several persons named in an RFP from whom you can get information:
- ☐ A Subject Matter Expert ( SME) who answers questions about specific requirements of the program.
- ☐ A program contact who can interpret the rules of the program or give you an indication if a project that you are thinking of would be allowable. It is recommended that you contact this person to be sure that your program fits the funder's priorities and that your program has a chance of being funded. Placing this call early can help you to adjust your program or change your project to meet the funder's needs.
- ☐ A support person or help desk that will assist you with getting your application completed or answering questions you may have
- ☐ A technical questions person who can assist when having problems using an online application process
- ☐ There may also be a person designated to receive the applications. This is especially true when you are using mailed applications.

www.HDGrants.com

If funded, is there a possibility of continuing funding after the award period expires?

☐ Many of the larger projects contemplated by public safety agencies are very expensive and must be broken up over several grants or several grant years by using a "phased approach". In some programs this is allowable and may be encouraged. Showing that you have success with one particular grant and then using that success as a building block for the next grant is often times a very successful technique.

☐ There are also programs where the eligibility is limited to only those agencies that had successfully completed one of these type programs or the same program in a different funding year.

Is there an application kit or package?

☐ Most Federal grants now use an on-line or "E-grants" application.

☐ Private and corporate programs may have these kits or hidden websites that you are given access codes to get into.

☐ Many States have their own grant application kits, which include copies of RFPs, specific reporting or application forms, etc.

### Due Dates/Deadlines

**❗ Must Do** — The number one rule of a successful grant application is do not miss the deadline! These deadlines are usually cast in stone and if you are even one minute late submitting, you are out of the running. You cannot win, if you do not play, and in order to play your application has to be submitted on time.

The proposal/application is due on what Date/Time?

**❗ Must Do** — Key Point # 3- Never miss the deadline!

☐ If you are applying using an E-grant, you should always allow ample time to submit. Never wait until the last day to submit an E-grant application.

☐ It is possible that the funding agencies server will experience problems close to the deadline due to the number of applications being submitted. In the 2005, Assistance to Firefighters Grant Program, the GMS server crashed for 14 hours on the last 24 hours of the grant application period!

☐ Your ISP (Internet Service Provider) server may go down, or the power grid may fail.

☐ Have an alternative plan of action so you do not miss a submission deadline.

## Step Two: You Found A Grant

If it says the deadline is 5:00PM EST and you live in a different time zone be sure to account for this. Most online applications simply have a turn off a button and at one minute after the deadline it is pre-programmed to shut itself off and not accept any more applications.

Does the deadline refer to the date your proposal must be in their hands? Or to the last date your package can be postmarked?

- ☐ There is a definite difference between these, and some programs may not accept a paper application.
- ☐ If the deadline refers to a postmark date, then you can take your package to the post office and have it stamped at the counter to ensure an accurate time stamp. However we recommend that you use a delivery service such as FED EX or UPS with guaranteed delivery as well as a signature at the time and date the package was delivered.
- ☐ If the deadline refers to the date your package must be received, be sure to allow ample time for the delivery service and or USPS to get it there.

*How should the proposal be delivered?*

- ☐ Unless otherwise required, you should always use a service that guarantees overnight delivery or hand deliver it yourself.
- ☐ On large grants, there have been instances where chartered aircraft have been used to hand deliver an application. That may sound a bit extreme, but when you are talking millions of dollars in grants that can make or break your agency, it quickly becomes a viable option if you have procrastinated too long.
- ☐ Be sure to obtain a receipt with a date and signature from the courier.
- ☐ Mailed applications should go USPS certified mail with a return receipt. Be sure to keep that paperwork with your permanent grant file, as it is your only proof of submittal. This is critical when you are applying to Foundations.

**4. Where should the proposal/application be mailed/delivered?**

- ☐ You will need a street address and telephone number if you are going to use UPS or FedEx.

They will not deliver to a P.O. Box.

- ☐ Remember to check if paper applications are acceptable (most are E-grant submissions today).

www.HDGrants.com     **63**

Grant Writer's Handbook

Use caution in reading this also as it is not unusual for paper applications to require being submitted to a different address than the program office itself.

### Funding Source Information

Most department's seeking a grant already have a specific thing in mind when they go after a grant. It may be a new squad car, equipment, or training money so they try searching for a grant using those parameters. This is a poor way to search for things. Grant funding sources all have funding priorities that the grant program was established to serve. Grants or funders are interesting in solving a problem within your community. Keep in mind that grants are not about getting stuff for your agency but solving a problem. When you are thinking of the equipment that you need think of what problem it creates when you don't have this equipment or what problem you will resolve by getting the equipment. Lack of radios is not a problem, lack of communication is the problem and radios will help to resolve this problem.

In private and corporate type grant programs the funding sources priorities may be for:

Community Development

Humanitarian Issues

Health Needs of Kids or Elderly

Education

Cultural Issues or Arts Support

Animal Rights

Human Rights

**! Must Do** The list can be wide and varied but regardless of who the funding source is, the successful grant writer must recognize that unless their program or request fits into those priorities, the proposal will not be supported or funded. It is imperative to form the nexus between the funding sources priorities and your own priorities first.

There is an old fly fisherman's mantra that is applicable here; "if you want to catch more fish then 'Match the Hatch'". When a fly fisherman arrives at a new fishing stream he looks for signs like insects landing on the water and the fish swirling up to eat them or he will cast around until landing a fish and then examine the contents of its stomach to see what is being devoured currently. The fly fisherman will then look into his own tackle box and try to find a similar fly lure to use. This usually always results in catching more fish.

## Step Two: You Found A Grant

A successful grant writer uses that same technique. Look for the clues as to what the funding source wants to eat, so to speak, and then make what you need, match what they wish to accomplish.

As an example let's say the priorities of the funding source say that they wish to "Increase the quality and level of medical care in rural areas for pediatric patients" and you are looking for a new ambulance for your rural VFD/Rescue department. If you read that programs RFP you will not find it stating that it will fund a new ambulance for you, however, if you examine that statement or priority you can make that work for you; here is why.

The goal of the funding source is to increase the quality and level of medical care in rural areas for pediatric patients, so let's step outside the box, look at that statement, and ask the following questions so that we can fit their goals and objectives. The questions would be:

Q-Are we serving a rural area?

A - Well yes, look at our name. The ABC Rural Volunteer Fire Department and Rescue Squad

Q-Are we part of the chain involved in delivering quality medical care?

A - It is no secret that the local ambulance or rescue squad is the very first link in delivering quality medical care to your citizens

Q-Do we transport children in our ambulance?

A - Why of course you transport children ( read "pediatric patients" here).

Now see, you have just fit yourself into that funding priority as an eligible provider of those type services and if a new ambulance is needed to be able to raise that level of quality medical care in your area, then it becomes a necessary part of your program to increase that level of medical care. Bingo, voila! The ambulance may have just become eligible as long as the RFP did not exclude vehicles elsewhere in the document.

---

This can be done with many, many projects if you simply step outside your world and examine the issue from a different perspective or from the funding source's point of view. This is a proven technique. Use it frequently and you will find that many more funding sources may become apparent to you.

Tips

---

Try to establish what the funding source is trying to accomplish with this grant program. Grants exist to solve specific identified problems, and those who address the priorities of the grant maker are the ones that get funded more frequently.

Remember

---

www.HDGrants.com                                                                                                        65

## Grant Writer's Handbook

Here is what to look for when reading the RFP:

1. **On what specific services or priorities is the RFP and funding source focusing?**
   - ☐ Look for the services they are prioritizing and applicable to your needs.
   - ☐ Solve the funding sources problem first and then your need,
   - ☐ What is the primary purpose of the grant program?
     - Your entire grant program should address that priority.
     - Remember most grants are program- or service-driven, not shopping list invitations.
   - ☐ Will funding your project fit their priorities? Can you state your need in relevant terms?
   - ☐ This is where you need the "out of the box" thinking we discussed earlier.
   - ☐ Articulate clearly how solving your problem is right in line with their mission.

2. **Which population, if any, is the funding source targeting?**
   - ☐ Are they looking at juveniles, senior citizens or minorities?
   - ☐ Must the targeted population fit a particular economic condition, such as 10% below the average median income?
   - ☐ Is there ethnic targeting involved?
   - ☐ Are there population caps in place that affect levels of funding or matching dollar requirements?
     - In the BVP grant (Bullet Proof Vest Partnership) those that are serving populations under 100K are afforded priority funding status.
     - The AFGP (Assistance to Firefighters Grant) determines the matching dollar requirement based on the population served).
     - The USDA Rural Facilities Grant Program will only build a new public safety building for those serving rural locations with populations under 20K

3. **Is the funding source focusing on a certain geographical area?**
   - ☐ Rural or Urban.
   - ☐ Tribal Lands
   - ☐ Hurricane–prone areas.
   - ☐ Major metropolitan areas.
   - ☐ Such as Urban Area Security Initiatives cities.
     - Large transit or port facilities.

## Step Two: You Found A Grant

4. **What are the criteria for approving the grant application?**
   - ☐ Will there be a computer screening to determine competitive range?
     - ■ The AFG uses this exclusively for determining competitive range and who goes on to the peer review panel.
   - ☐ Is there a minimum number of program priorities, which you must address?
   - ☐ Sometimes there is a requirement to meet at least two out of three priorities to be awarded funding.
   - ☐ Sometimes the more priorities you address, the higher funding priority you attain. That means extra points for your application.

5. **What are the funding priorities? Are there high and low priorities?**

---

Increase your chances of being funded by focusing on the highest priorities of the funding agency.

Tips

- ☐ If you mix low priority items with high priority items, it will lower the overall score of your grant. Grants are usually awarded from highest scoring to lowest scoring until the funding source runs out of money. Grant scoring and funding can be decided by as little as .25% of a point; you need every percentage of a point you can gain for your application. Here is how that works.

If the priorities of the program state that higher consideration will be given to those applicants seeking funding for equipment which will "increase officer safety" this is how that would play out in scoring using a 1-5 scale with 5 being the highest score.

If you asked for bullet proof vests they would score 5

Traffic Safety Vests would score at 5

Flashlights would score about 3, (even though it could be argued that it is an officer safety item)

The total average score for your grant would be 5+5+3= 13 divided by 3 = 4.3. Average score. If you had left the flashlights out of the grant, it would have scored 5+5 = 10 divided by 2 = 5. That 5 score will be funded ahead of you. Keep lower scoring items out of the grant if the other items are more critical to be awarded. That .7 difference could be the difference between an award letter and a rejection notice.

- ☐ Look for information as to how the grant will be reviewed or evaluated such as: "We will rank all complete and eligible applications based on the substance of your application relative to the established program priorities. Applications that best address

www.HDGrants.com

## Grant Writer's Handbook

the grant program's priorities will score higher than those applications that are not directed toward the priorities."

Using the recent Public Safety Interoperable Communications grant program as an example, the panelists will typically evaluate and score:

1. The clarity and comprehensiveness of your proposed project including your project's budget detail and how well your proposal matches the funding sources priorities

2. The financial need of your organization,

3. The cost benefits that would result should you be awarded the grant, and

4. The extent to which the grant would enhance your daily operations and/or how the grant will positively impact your ability to protect life and property.

These four elements carry equal weight when factored into the review panelists' scores (i.e., one-fourth).

In this example, then, your proposal would use four headings:

1. Project Description and Proposed Project

2. Financial Need

3. Cost Benefits

4. Statement of Effect on Daily Operational Outcomes

5. What are the goals of the funding source?
- ☐ A goal is a specific event that must occur, such as "lowering the number of severe, injury accidents."
- ☐ What is the grant source seeking to do?
- ☐ Lower the rate of injuries.
- ☐ Raise public awareness.
- ☐ Reduce property losses due to fire.
- ☐ Improve communications between different agencies
- ☐ Who are they trying to help?
- ☐ The goal of many grant programs in the public safety sector is "to enhance the safety of officers"
- ☐ Identify victims of domestic violence.

## Step Two: You Found A Grant

Your goals must match the funding sources' goals. Make sure you include the same wording (parrot the language) the funding source uses in the guidelines. Goals are often stated in very specific terms and are clearly identifiable. However, it might not specifically spell out what the goals are and the goal could be "disguised within other language" so you must be able to discern this subtlety. Some of the language we have encountered when describing the goals of the programs have been worded like this:

Must Do

"Describe your agency's mission to disrupt the illicit drug market in your community."

"Will the equipment requested enhance mutual aid or interoperability with other agencies based upon the NIMS criteria in place?"

"Describe the financial need of your organization and elaborate on the benefits your community and/or organization will gain from the expenditure of the grant funds, particularly noting the benefits that would be realized due to your department's responsibilities for protection of critical infrastructure."

When the grant reviewer is scanning the applications to determine which ones they must read and score, they will look for "keywords" like "Interoperability" or "interagency cooperation" and highlight them because their instructions for funding someone have stated the "the grant must encourage interoperability and interagency cooperation". As a result, we have known grant reviewers who actually go back and count the number of highlighted words and use that as screening criteria in determining which grants they will actually read or not read thoroughly.

Remember the reviewers get these words directly from the RFP. Write your grant proposal using the language in the RFP this will insure that the reviewers will get exactly what they are looking for.

### *Proposal Sections*
1. **What is the total number of sections required?**
   - ☐ What are the specific names of each section?
   - ☐ These sections are determined by headings and questions in the application, or as in the example above, how the grant will be evaluated.
   - ☐ Are there size limitations in these individual sections like numbers, words, or page limitations?
   - ☐ This is a key element in the new E-grant age. If you are required to have 1" margins, or no more than 2500 characters, the computer may not accept your application if items don't match or exceed set limits. This means your grant may never make it to the review

# Grant Writer's Handbook

process. It might also result in just accepting what the character or word count limit is and then simply deleting anything beyond that. The reviewer would be reading and might only get 4 pages of a 5 page narrative leaving them hanging without seeing that final data that triggers their decision to fund or not fund you. Be careful about this, it is a critical mistake and leads to many rejections because the writer did not make sure everything that they wrote was successfully uploaded and accepted by the database. Read carefully!

2. **How does the funding source want the information organized?**

   ☐ Even though the grant application guidelines sometimes require that you present your proposal in a specific way, you should write your proposal in an orderly manner, and then reorganize the components as requested in the grant application.

Clues to this can be discerned by paying attention to exactly what is being said, For example this language below is quoted directly from a Federal grant application:

*\* Please provide your narrative statement in the space provided below. Include in your narrative, details regarding (1) your project's description and budget, (2) your organization's financial need, (3) the benefit to be derived from the cost of your project, and (4) how the activities requested in your application will help your organization's daily operations and how this grant will protect life and property.*

As you can clearly see the program has specifically spelled out what they want to appear and what you must discuss in the narrative section of the grant application. Pay attention to what is listed after each (1), (2), (3), (4) and note the order in which it is presented. This is exactly how you should set up your narrative using the language after each numeral as the header title for each of the four sections of the narrative.

This is one of those things where you have to "read between the lines" to get your application just right. Always remember that how you read and interpret the guidelines, or RFP, is a direct reflection of your agencies ability to "follow directions" and be a good steward of the funding sources money. If they see that you missed a clear instruction such as this, what would they likely think about your ability to follow directions in handling a $100K award they are thinking about giving you?

Key Point #4 - Failure to follow directions is the #1 reason that grants get denied and rejected.

3. **What information will I need to answer each section set out in the RFP?**

   ☐ What statistical data do I need to answer this question?
   ☐ Where will I locate this data or who will provide it for me?

## Step Two: You Found A Grant

Tips

One of the most basic rules of grant writing is to always be sure to clearly answer the question that is asked. Sometimes a simple "yes or no" is all you need. Supplying sufficient and detailed data to answer the question is called for but use caution that you don't shoot yourself in the foot by going too far in your answer. Pick and choose your wording carefully. Be thorough but resist the urge to further embellish your answer.

What I am referring to is best explained by looking at a question that appears on the USSTC/Polaris Corporate grant application to give a Polaris Ranger to a public safety agency. The question asked simply states," Does your organization currently own an ATV?"

We have seen a number of grant applicants answer that question by stating, "No, we currently have to borrow one from one of our members when needed?"

This grant writer just shot themselves in the foot with that answer because, the grant program seeks to place these vehicles with those organizations who simply do NOT have one. By embellishing what should have been a simple answer of "no" to that question the writer stated that even though they did not have one, they could borrow one from a member of their department. They just greatly diminished their need by doing that.

4. Do I understand what is requested in each section?

☐ If not, what do I need to do or who do I need to call to clarify?

Create an outline with the main points that should be included in each section. It is very important to repeat the main points in your proposal almost exactly as they are written or appear in the RFP. This is called "parroting the language". It lets the reviewer know that you have studied and read the RFP thoroughly and understand what they are trying to accomplish with the program - and you are forming that nexus between their need and your need.

### Support

1. Do I have support from my administrators, council, or director?

This is one of the first things to determine. If they are not behind your project then you should not waste time writing the proposal.

Remember

Sit your administrators and board members down prior to beginning your applications and be certain that you thoroughly discuss their concerns and that you have "buy-in" from them. Their post-award support will be critical in administering and successfully implementing and completing your grant program thereby fulfilling your obligation to do so with the funding source.

It also pre-empts the possibility, which we see frequently happening, of wasting all your precious time and effort at developing a comprehensive grant application only to take it before the Chief for a final signature approval to be told, "this is not what I wanted and mitigating the decision to quickly add something into the grant in the 11th hour before deadline. This is a sure-fire way to get a rejection notice.

2. **Who will provide signatures for the grant? Will they be available? Keep in mind most Foundation grants are still paper grants.**

☐ We have spent countless hours writing an application only to find out that the person who needs to sign off on the proposal is out of town.

Count on Murphy's Law – it will get you every time. We have found it usually better to seek these signatures at the very beginning of your process so that you will not have to find that person as the deadline approaches

3. **Arrange for others to read the RFP and ask, sincerely, for their support and input. There are basically three different types of proofreading and feedback that you're looking for.**

☐ Have people in your field read it for content. They may notice critical details you've missed.

☐ Ask people outside your field, preferably of varying educational backgrounds, to read your story. Here, you're looking for validation that you've compellingly stated your need for the funds and explained comprehensively and with sufficient detail that the common citizen understands. If these readers are convinced, you have done your job as a grant writer. If, on the other hand, they seem perplexed by what they are reading this is something you should address immediately and revise or clarify.

☐ Finally, you need a skilled writer, like an English teacher or a newspaper editor, to give you a very detailed proofread, correcting grammar, spelling, phrasing, and even checking the math in the budget.

Format – many people fail to grasp the significance of formatting in a grant application. They think it is minutia or irrelevant but this is an often fatal error that grant writers make. It is critical for a number of reasons which can range from the funding source scanning the documents into a computer, or for an archiving or reproduction reason or to distribute to reviewers via email and for other reasons as well. One of the most frequently ignored reasons but, probably the single most important reason to pay close attention to this is that it can be used as a screening technique by the finding source to determine if you are following directions.

## Step Two: You Found A Grant

1. **How many copies should be sent to the funding source?**
   - ☐ You should always print the requested number of copies directly from your computer, as opposed to using a photocopier (they will be cleaner and neater).

   Use good quality paper with decent weight 22-24 lb and 93%+ brightness factor. This is not the time to use the local office supply store special of the week or routine paper supply that resides in your printer.

   - ☐ Mark the original with a removable note or in the manner that the RFP suggests
   - ☐ Have the original signed in "blue" ink so that it is clearly distinguishable as the original.

   ---
   *Do not use colored papers or colored ink. This is a business document and color is usually not appropriate. It should be a b/w document.* — Tips
   ---

2. **Is there a restriction on the font and pitch?**
   - ☐ Use Times New Roman, 12 point, if not otherwise stipulated.

   ---
   *It is a good idea in eGrant applications to see if you can go into the narrative area and write a few lines and then print it out to see if formatting holds and what size and font will be printed for the reviewer. You need to see exactly what the reviewer is going to have in their hands and make adjustments accordingly.* — Tips
   ---

   We have seen some resident databases used to store grant applications, or accept them, that will take quotation marks and turn them into upside down question marks or that will not accept a bullet point and then scramble everything after it. Tables are particularly bad about transferring incorrectly. Be sure your formatting will hold and print correctly.

3. **How should the proposal be prepared, organized, and packaged?**
   - ☐ Stapled, bound, paper clip etc.

   Should it be original with 4 copies under it or vice versa? Look for clues on how they want it presented to them.

4. **What are the margin restrictions?**
   - ☐ Top, bottom and left and right.

   If it says 1 inch margins on side and 1.5 inch on sides and you do not discern this and put 1 inch margins all around; it can result in the grant not even being accepted and given to a reviewer to review.

5. **Is it best to "fully justify" your margins?**
   - ☐ Straight on left and right sides.

www.HDGrants.com

### Grant Writer's Handbook

6. What is the maximum number of pages the grant will allow in each section?
   - ☐ Does that number include graphs and charts?
   - ☐ Does the RPF state maximum number of pages, words, or characters?
   - ☐ Are the "attachments" or "assurances" counted in the total?
   - If it calls for a separate budget and narrative are they being counted in the total?

7. How and where should the grant pages be numbered?
   - ☐ Top or bottom.
   - ☐ Centered, left or right.

8. What types of forms or assurance documentation do I need? Where do I get them?
   - ☐ Tax returns
   - ☐ IRS letters of 501c(3) status
   - ☐ Assurances
   - ☐ EEO policies
   - ☐ MOUs (Memorandums of Understanding) or Letters of Support

**Checklist** — This checklist has been created to help you decide if the grant funding opportunity you find is really for your organization. If you answer "no" to any of the areas, STOP and reconsider pursuing this specific grant funding opportunity.

| Guiding Questions to Qualify Funders | Yes | No |
|---|---|---|
| Is my agency eligible to apply (all types of funders)? | | |
| When is the deadline for the application and can we meet it (all types of funders)? | | |
| Does the grant meet the funding priorities that we established in our planning process (all types of funders)? | | |
| Is this a service or activity my agency is equipped to implement (all types of funders)? | | |
| Will there be more than 10 grant awards (state and federal funders)? | | |
| Is the maximum grant award enough to fund at least 50% or more of the project budget (all types of funders)? | | |
| Is there a geographic restriction (all types of funders)? | | |
| Does our idea for a grant request match the funder's guidelines and interest (all types of funders)? | | |

# 5. Step Three: The Grant Proposal

## Components of a Grant

In the following chapters, we discuss the components that are included in a successful grant proposal. Not all of these components would be included in every proposal, but it gives you an idea of what items you need to be discussing.

Many of these headings will be sections or requirements of the RFP or grant guidelines. Even if they are not main headings, you should incorporate each of these somewhere in your grant or concept paper. It may only take a sentence or two in a short concept paper, but in a more complex paper, you may devote an entire section to each of these components. As each of these sections is discussed in detail, you will see why they are important to your overall grant proposal.

The main sections seen in grant applications and proposals are:

- ☐ Project Summary
- ☐ Problem Statement/Need Statement
- ☐ Program Approach/Project Description
- ☐ Cost Benefit
- ☐ Goals and Objectives
- ☐ Evaluation/Operational Outcomes
- ☐ Management Plan or Timeline
- ☐ Sustainability

**Performance Measures**

- ☐ Exportable Products
- ☐ Conclusion
- ☐ Budget

When you begin writing the actual grant proposal or narrative sections, be sure to use a word processing program and 'save' frequently. This decreases the chances of losing the

# Grant Writer's Handbook

document permanently, and it will be much easier to edit and distribute to consultants and others on your grant team. Plus, with the E-grants process, you can copy and paste your narrative in the appropriate section on the GMS system. One word of caution: GMS only gives you one chance to hit the submit button, so do not cut and paste anything until you're ready to submit everything. Many online applications have "time out" features and if you get up and walk away from your application while logged in it will automatically log you out however, you may not know it has logged you out. Be cautious of this happening. Lastly, when e-mailing your proposal, always send it as a separate file attached to your e-mail message. Don't paste your narrative into the body of the e-mail.

## *Project Summary*

The project summary should be a brief overview of your entire grant application, containing concise statements to introduce the reader to the substance of your proposal. The project summary is one of the first ways to bond with the reader and is similar to an abstract or overview section, found at the beginning of most grant proposals.

**Tips**

While the reviewers will read this section first, you should write it last. Why? Because your ability to bring focus and clarity to your project, will be greater at the end of the process than it is at the beginning. You may even find that the summary practically writes itself.

### Outlining the Project Summary

Begin by deciding on what things you would want to include in this section to get the reviewer interested in your program. Consider the following questions and comments.

1. What needs to be in my project summary?

2. The project summary should mention key parts of your proposal. What are the key elements in your proposal? What should the reviewer know about your program?

3. Consider the main parts that you mention in the project summary (list a main point from your proposal beside each one). Your parts may be different depending on the type of grant and the RFP.

**Checklist**

- ☐ Purpose and overall goal of the grant proposal.
- ☐ Setting or location of your program.
- ☐ Identifies the problem.
- ☐ Target population or geographic area.

## Step Three: The Grant Proposal

- ☐ List of program activities.
- ☐ Exportable product.
- ☐ Evaluation.
- ☐ Summary statement.

### Writing the Project Summary

Using your outline above, begin writing the project summary. Remember to be concise and to the point. Use the following examples to write your project summary.

1. Begin this section with the purpose or goal of the grant. Remember to use your program name or title.

This will help personalize your program to those reviewing it.

- ☐ The purpose of [program name] is to . . .
- ☐ The goal of [program name] is to . . .

I.E: The purpose of the Washington Park Safe Streets project is to eliminate or curtail the sale of illicit narcotics within the Washington Park's area of our City.

2. Briefly state what the problem is without going into the causes or long-term effects.

- ☐ The problem is that ...
- ☐ This program addresses the problem of . . .

I.E: This program addresses the problem of street level sales of illicit narcotics by youth gangs, in what the citizens of the area have are describing as a "Drug Supermarket" hot spot .

3. Describe the target population and say why they were selected. This could be tied into the statement above.

- ☐ The target population or target area will include . . .
- ☐ This program will target ...

I.E: This program will target the Hispanic youth gang members frequenting this area and engaging in narcotics sales to drive-thru vehicular traffic.

4. Next, list some of the basic activities of your program approach. You may want to use your outline created in the program approach section (Chapter 5) to generate a list of activities. Do not go into any detail. Just state the program activities.

- ☐ The project will include . . .

www.HDGrants.com 77

## Grant Writer's Handbook

☐ Program activities will include . . .

☐ The activities of this program will consist of the following . . .

IE: This program will form and deploy a street crimes unit within our police department who will be running undercover street drug buys and developing intelligence for drug search warrants and arrest and prosecution for these crimes.

5. State what the exportable product(s) will be in concise terms.

☐ The exportable products will be . . .

☐ . . . will be developed as a result of this program

☐ This program will export knowledge through . . .

I.E: During these operations information developed through arrests and other sources of intelligence will be entered into a centralized countywide gang intelligence database.

☐ Outline how you will evaluate your program.

- This program will be independently evaluated by . . .
- An evaluation will be conducted to . . .

IE: At the conclusion of this program and at routine periods throughout, the effectiveness of the program will be gauged by # of arrests and comparison of complaints by residents of observed street sales of narcotics.

7. Finally, provide a wrap-up sentence that leaves the reader with a good feeling. Remember to not end this section abruptly. You may want to mention the name of your program again. End it on a positive note!

☐ This program will not solve all of our problems but . . .

☐ As a result of this program, . . .

☐ This program will be the first step . . .

I.E: This project is the first of several of pro-active steps being undertaken by our department to return the streets to a safe condition in this neighborhood so that the residents may walk and live without fear.

### Project Summary Checklist

Below are some things to check for after writing your project summary.

## Step Three: The Grant Proposal

**Checklist**

- ☐ Begins with the purpose or goal of the grant.
- ☐ The project summary is not wordy, but concise.
- ☐ No extraneous detail.
- ☐ Briefly outlines the setting.
- ☐ Defines the target population and why they were selected.
- ☐ Outlines specific program activities.
- ☐ Informs the reader what the problem is (not causes and long-term effects).
- ☐ Tells what the exportable product(s) will be.
- ☐ Outlines the project evaluation.
- ☐ Provides a wrap-up or a transition statement that leaves the reader with a good feeling.

### Problem/Needs Statement

**Tips**

As a grant writer, you should think of yourself as a combination of an award winning photojournalist and author. Many failed grant proposals are in essence, black and white photographs that lack definition or clarity. It is your job to immerse the reader into your community, department, environment, and problems. You need to provide the reader with an 8 x 10, color, glossy photograph. You provide this photograph through your words.

Think about the last time you read a good book or magazine article. What was it that captivated you and kept you reading that book till 5:00AM when you had only intended to read for a few minutes till you dozed off? Could you picture the places and people the author was describing? Could you put yourself in their situation and feel their happiness? Their sadness? Their fear or excitement?

**Remember**

The successful author makes it easy for you to identify with their characters and the places and events that are occurring as the story is told. The successful grants writer does the same thing, but in a condensed format. You must grab the reviewer's attention and keep it focused, from start to finish, on what you are telling them. Reviewers should never have to lift their eyes from your grant narrative from the time they begin reading it, until the time they read the last word. Your grant proposal should compel the reviewer to want to help your community or to help resolve the particular problem you present.

**Must Do**

Reviewer's usually have only a very limited amount of time to read your grant and literally hundreds of applications to score. In Federal grant programs there can be 20K+ applications. One reviewer can be scoring 100 applications in a single day; that works out to about only 6 minutes per application. They may be doing that for 3-4 days during the grant review process and believe me, they get tired and grumpy. It is, therefore, critical to make their job as easy as possible; do not do things that are likely to irritate the reviewer. Imagine

www.HDGrants.com

how tired or "ready to get it over with" you might feel at the end of the day and then imagine that your grant is the 399th one that the reviewer has looked at.

### Rule #1 - don't irritate the reviewer!

Do not make the mistake of assuming that just because you filled in a box at the beginning of the grant with some piece of information, that you should not mention this information within your narrative and here is why.

Think about reading a good newspaper story appearing on the front page. You are thoroughly engaged in the story and reading along for several columns and then it suddenly ends and says "continued on page 7". Does that not irritate you? What usually happens while turning to page 7? Something else distracts you and you read it, right? Then you eventually make it to page 7 and must return to page 1 and read several lines to get back on track, right?

How long did that take you to accomplish? I bet it took 30-60 seconds, if you are fast. Make a reviewer do that even 3-4 times and he or she is going to lose precious critical time and interest needed to actually read your narrative and they will become unfocused on your application. Frustration sets in and they will put your grant down and seek one that does not make them do that.

This is why it is important to know who exactly is going to be reading your grant and what the process will be like for them. You need to identify and know the target audience reading your work. Is it a spouse of a Fortune 500 executive who sits on their Foundation Board and has a degree from an Ivy League College or a Volunteer Fire Chief from the plains of North Dakota with nothing but a high school diploma who left his 5000 acre wheat farm for the first time just to come to Emmitsburg, MD to read your Assistance to Firefighters Grant?

You must always keep the reviewer's perspective at the top of your mind as you think through your problem statement. If you are going to make a statement and that statement raises or begs another question in order to further clarify it, then your very next statement should do that. They are not allowed to pick up a phone and call you to get clarification on something. The reviewer should have zero questions about your program when they are finished reading your proposal.

Here's where the fact that you know your problems inside and out can actually work against you. Remember, your reviewer has never heard this story and you must fill in critical details that you automatically assume everyone else knows. Familiarity breeds contempt. Step outside that box and remember that the reviewer may possibly have never set foot outside of his own county, in his own state. Yes I know that seems rather unlikely in this day and age

## Step Three: The Grant Proposal

but, the fact remains that it is the truth and you cannot run the risk of not taking that into consideration. You must provide that level of detail, or colorization", to make a B/W story become an 8X10 color glossy.

Most review panels involve multiple reviewers reading your grant. This is usually 3-5 people and you must win a majority vote of approval from them to receive an award. That means that there is always one person on that panel that is the "swing vote"; lose that vote and you fail. This is why you have to try to hedge your bets here and make sure that you do not leave any piece of pertinent information out of your narrative.

Many people will tell you to keep the narrative "short and concise". We have found through interviewing reviewers that the ones who usually make those statements were first time reviewers who did not understand what they were being asked to do until they arrived to sit on a panel. They signed up for something which requires a love of reading and good comprehensive reading skills and they simply do not have them. They were poor readers to begin with and do not read for enjoyment, or even daily, so reading 400 applications of 5-6 pages each becomes too much like work for them and they get frustrated at their own lack of reading skills.

We are here to tell you that there is a big difference between short and concise. If it takes you 5 pages of single spaced typing to tell your story completely and in great detail and you do so without repeating yourself or being redundant, then it is concise at 5 pages. You cannot run the risk of leaving out a key piece of detailed information that might just be the key point that sways that final swing vote that you need. "Different strokes for different folks", comes to mind here. What is important to one reviewer may have little value to another. The trick here is that a reviewer can skip that information if they don't feel it is important but, they cannot read something important to them if you leave it out! Chances are the swing vote is going to be someone with great reading skills who enjoys what they are doing and that my friend, is the one person you need to impress most because he/she is likely to argue in favor of you for funding and will convince the others that you have all the elements necessary to receive the funding.

This section will help you organize your problem statement to grab the reader's attention. It is important to have a detailed, concise statement defining the problems, causes, and long-term impacts. The problem statement should instill a sense of urgency in the reader, while compelling the reviewer to want to help you solve your problem. You want the reviewer to feel like they have an extraordinary opportunity to solve an important problem by funding your program. To accomplish this you must use statistics but it is also very helpful to use examples. If space permits, citing an incident in your community will have an emotional impact on the

### Grant Writer's Handbook

reviewer and helps to prove you have a problem but it also puts the problem in human terms. Reviewers can clearly see how your situation or problem is effecting the community.

One of the best ways to begin this process is with an outline. Just get your thoughts down on paper. You will find it much easier to extend these thoughts into complete sentences, then you can review, and edit the document as need be.

Sample Outline

*Problem Statement*

1. Who are you?

2. Where are you?

3. Who do you serve?

4. What is the exact problem?

5. Why do you have this problem?

6. Who is affected by this problem?

7. What have you done to try to fix it already?

8. What will happen long term if nothing is done?

*Needs Assessment/Defining The Problem*

The first purpose of the needs assessment is to define the problem, causes and symptoms. Ask these questions.

1. What are the gaps in the successful, effective, and efficient programs, services, and needs?

2. What is lacking in the current methods of dealing with a situation or delivery of service?

3. What are the barriers?

4. What are the origins of this problem? How did it get to this point? What are the causes?

5. How do I know this problem exists? What are the symptoms?

6. What will happen if nothing is done about this problem?

7. What is already functioning well? What resources do I already have? List your strengths.

## Step Three: The Grant Proposal

Decide what the problem is and consider these questions.

1. Who will benefit? The target population or geographic area is the recipient of a program or project. This group or area is the focus, to reduce the effects of the problem. What is the primary and secondary target population or geographic area?

2. How will they benefit?

3. How long will it take?

4. How much will it cost?

5. How will you sustain it?

6. What is the area you are targeting? (This is usually a geographic area or focus location, such as a school.)

7. What is the area for the target population? What area am I trying to serve?

One of the easier ways of doing this, is by employing the SARA model. This is a problem solving model that can be used to address any problem. The SARA model has four states; Scanning, Analysis, Response and Assessment. The SARA model is not the only way to approach a problem, but it can serve as a helpful tool.

Tips

### Scanning
- ☐ Analyzing calls for service.
- ☐ Incident data.
- ☐ Other agency records for patterns and trends.
- ☐ Mapping according to time of day, location and other similar factors.
- ☐ Consulting officers, supervisors, mid-level managers, and command staff.
- ☐ Reviewing reports.
- ☐ Surveying community residents, businesses, elected officials, or targeted groups.
- ☐ Participating in community meetings.
- ☐ Reviewing information from organizations (local and national).
- ☐ Consulting government agencies.
- ☐ Media coverage.

# Grant Writer's Handbook

## 2. Analysis

Comprehensively analyzing a problem is critical to the success of a problem-solving effort. Effective, tailor-made responses cannot be developed unless you know what is causing the problem. You must resist the urge to skip the analysis phase, or you run the risk of addressing a problem that doesn't exist and/or implementing solutions that are ineffective in the long run. The first step in analysis is to determine what information is needed. This should be a broad inquiry, uninhibited by past perspectives; questions should be asked; regardless of whether or not answers can be obtained.

Consider the crime triangle.

Generally, three elements are required to constitute a crime: an offender, a victim and a crime scene or location. As part of the analysis phase, it is important to find out as much as possible about all three legs of the triangle. One way is to start by asking who, what, when, where, why and why not regarding each leg of the triangle.

Law enforcement officers will relate this to writing an investigative report. Who will be reading your report—the Sergeant, Chief, State Attorney, Defense Attorney, the Judge, or the Jury, before they decide the fate of a suspect? What is it that we want to try to answer for the reader before they actually have to think about it? You must try to anticipate the reader's questions. Try using these as a guide for your thought and analysis.

**Victim:** Research shows that a small number of victims account for a large amount of incidents.

**Offender:** It is helpful to learn more about why offenders are attracted to certain victims and places, what specifically they gain by offending, and what, if anything could prevent or reduce their rates of offending.

**Location:** Research again shows that certain locations account for a significant amount of all criminal activity. An analysis of these locations may indicate why they are so conducive to a

## Step Three: The Grant Proposal

particular crime or problem and point to ways in which they can be altered, resolved, lessened, or inhibited. Looking for patterns in whatever problem you are trying to solve will help you in identifying or justifying the solution.

### 3. Response

We are constantly battling a natural tendency to revert to traditional responses. It is only natural that we will gravitate toward the same tactics that we have used in the past, to address problems in the future - even if these tactics have not been especially effective or sustainable over the long-term. The key to developing tailored responses is making sure the responses are very focused and directly linked to the finding from the analysis phase of the project. Don't be afraid to buck tradition.

---

Grants traditionally seek to offer a unique solution, to unique problems, in a unique community. They constantly are seeking the "better mousetrap". Faster, more efficient, bigger bang for the buck and improved safety are things that these programs seek to fund constantly. Developing a method or techniques of solving a problem that is easily replicable is also what they seek here, so other departments can implement your gained knowledge or a better way of doing things. Bear that in mind when you are developing this model.

Tips

---

### 4. Assessment

Many times the assessment phase is a repeat of the analysis phase, with notations of the changes.

This is good information to use in the evaluation section of the grant, which we will talk about later in this book. If the responses implemented are not effective, the information gathered during analysis should be reviewed. New information may need to be collected before new solutions can be developed and tested.

The second purpose of the needs assessment is to gather data to prove and determine the extent of your need and problem.

1 What types of data do I need to outline the problem?

2 What evidence and information demonstrate that there is a problem?

- This is where your statistical data is going to come into play.

3. What are the common types of data that I should collect to substantiate the need problem, like calls for service, arrests, per capita income, population below poverty, fire damage losses, fire burn injuries and deaths, crime rate, level of education, single-parent

www.HDGrants.com 85

### Grant Writer's Handbook

families, school dropouts, unemployment, homelessness, poverty, mental illness, alcohol and other drug abuse. Where possible, compare these figures to state or national statistics.

- Remember, never quote a statistic without providing the source of the statistic.

Provide studies and literature that add emphasis to the problem.

Use examples that are compelling and clearly show that your problem exists in your community.

If you are asking for equipment you may need to conduct a detailed inventory seeking out the dates of manufacture, age, mileage on trucks, quantity of items you have as compared to recommended levels and similar type information depending upon what you may be asking for.

Consider sources where you can acquire data to determine the need.

1. Where can I go to find out more about the problem? Seek out reports from FBI, IAFC, NFPA, NCJIS or other recognized authorities or standard setting organizations.

2. Who can I ask about the needs and problems? Who is the expert?

3. What are the different approaches I could take? What methods should I use?

4. Popular sources for data: Chamber of Commerce, school district, health department, United States Census Bureau, American Fact Finder, police and sheriff's records, fire department and town hall.

- You will find links to many of the most commonly used sources of this data, at www.hdgrnats.com under "Grants Resources".

5. Conduct surveys and questionnaires with relevant people.

### II. Writing The Problem Statement

Begin organizing your material and writing the problem statement by working from your outline. You can use your outline to effectively expand upon your ideas forming a problem statement.

Start by introducing your agency and telling where you are located. Explain who you serve, and include statistics that will describe your community and the population you serve.

## Step Three: The Grant Proposal

> * NOTE - You should keep in mind that the reader might not know where you are located. The number one subject failed by most high school seniors in the US is geography. It is important that you geographically orient the reviewer to where you are. Help them understand your problem and community better.

Tips

Depending upon the type of program and who the funding source is, this may be a simple one paragraph statement or it could require a more detailed statement if it was a major DHS grant program.

In a major DHS grant program such as the Assistance to Firefighters Grant the introductory statement would appear something like this:

The Alum Bank district is comprised of approximately a 150 square mile area of rural Bedford County in Pennsylvania with a population of 6511 residents, according to figures obtained from the 2000 US census. Our primary coverage area lies between the summit of the eastern front of the Appalachian Mountains and Interstate 99. Most everyone will remember our area as being 15 miles from the tragic scene where United Airlines Flight # 93 crashed on 9/11.

It is mostly a farming and residential area with one industrial park located within its boundaries. We provide automatic mutual aid to 6 departments spanning three counties. They include the Imler, Shawnee Valley, Windber, Claysburg, Bedford, and Everett fire departments. When taking automatic aid into consideration, we respond to an area of over 1200 square miles with a population of 30,809 residents.

The ABC Fire Company was formed in 1949 after a large fire destroyed a church in the area. The Bedford Fire Department was the closest company to this fire prior to the formation of our department and still serves as one of our automatic aid departments. The ABCFC protects 19- churches, 4- schools, 2- post offices, 1- bank, 5- medical care facilities, 7- restaurants, and 3- gas stations.

The Alum Bank Community Fire Company is an all-volunteer department with 29 members operating out of one station. Although 27% of these members are certified through the state by the NPQSB or IFSAC, it is required that all members receive training equivalent to NFPA 1001 prior to assuming an active role in this department. Such training is approved by the state of Pennsylvania and includes a 166 hour entry level Fire Training Program, a Structure Burn Program and a Hazardous Material Response Program. The active members of the Alum Bank Fire Department are NIMS compliant with the exception of two probationary members who are in the process of receiving such training.

www.HDGrants.com

Grant Writer's Handbook

In 2008, we responded to 153 calls. The breakdown of these calls is as follows: -39 Structure Fires, -5 Vehicle Fires, -11 Brush Fires, -47 Motor Vehicle Accidents, -16 EMS Assists, -4 Weather Related, -14 Good Intent/Automatic Alarms, - 8 Medivac Landing Zones, and -9 Other/Special Incidents. Our department responds to these emergencies using the following apparatus:

1994 Saulsbury Pumper 750 gal / 1250 gpm, mileage 51,474, seats 6

1978 Hendrickson Pumper 750 gal / 1500 gpm, mileage 25,069 on cab, seats 6

1- 1995 Freightliner Squad, mileage 111,251, seats 7

2009 Spartan Tanker 3000 gal / 750 gpm, mileage, seats 6

1975 Ford Bean 4x4 Brush 500 gal/ 66 gpm High Pressure, mileage 16372, seats 2

1987 Chevrolet 4x4 Brush 120 gal/ portable pump skid unit, mileage 127,563, seats 2

The ABC Fire Company provides service to the West St. Clair, East St. Clair, Napier, and Lincoln Townships as well as Pleasantville and New Paris Boroughs. We also serve as one of only four rapid intervention teams in Bedford County with eighteen of our members being trained at the advanced RIT level. This team is being dispatched on the first alarm with all of our automatic aid departments as well as departments in our surrounding counties. Our department is also requested to assist with motor vehicle accidents, fire extinguishment, salvage, and overhaul with these departments.

Next, state the problem that clearly defines your problem – exactly what you are trying to deal with

I.E: The problem is that we are experiencing an increase in crimes being reported in residential neighborhoods during the late afternoons between the hours of 3PM and 6PM.

The next sentence should define the cause(s) of the problem.

*The causes of the problem are, these crimes are being committed by "latchkey kids" whose dual income parents are working and they are being left unsupervised with idle time on their hands and no parental supervision*

Also, tell the reader what you have done to resolve this problem and what might happen if left un-checked.

## Step Three: The Grant Proposal

*Long-term, without intervention, we will see an increase in the severity of crimes being committed by these juveniles and at some point a homeowner will overreact and more than likely shoot and kill one of these juveniles when surprised by the homeowner while committing one of these burglaries.*

Center your discussion around the problem. Use your needs assessment and the data you have gathered to show your need.

---

It is also a good idea to have a thesaurus handy. Use the following to demonstrate the severity of your problem: worst, highest, lowest, less than, bottom, dependent, below, almost, failed, distressed, poor(est), plagued, trapped, desperate, grim, high-risk, hopeless, substandard, inadequate, pathetic, miserable, sparse, needy, destitute, poverty, neglect, disruption, barrier, disadvantaged, deficit, severe, depressed, lacking, unacceptable, minimum, impaired, widespread, discouraged, disheartened, hurdle, obstacle, violent, harsh, pitiful, miserable, ignore, outbreak, bleak, gloomy, overlooked, disregarded, increased, decreased, infested, etc...

Tips

### Hints For Writing Each Category

---

☐ 1. Include compelling statistics in each category that support the problem, its cause, and the long-term effects.
☐ 2. Statistics should come from a variety of sources. Re-read your problem statement several times
☐ 3. The problem statement focuses on the urgency of your problem.
☐ 4. The problem is proven and convinces the reader that it is serious and growing.
☐ 5. The problem statement does not include program activities.
☐ 6. The problem statement does not discuss the amount of funding needed.
☐ 7. Statistics are not spelled out and real whole numbers are used.
☐ 8. References to sources of information are made whenever a statistic is used.
☐ 9. Use a combination of narrative and bullets to explain the problem.
☐ 10. Graphics, graphs or charts are included as space permits.

Checklist

Conclude the problem section with a wrap-up statement that provides an overview of the problem and leads the reviewer into the approach section.

---

Re-read your problem statement several times. You need to compel the reader to want to provide money to solve your problem.

Must Do

Finally, be sure that you have correctly identified the actual problem and are not simply describing symptoms of the problem.

www.HDGrants.com

Grant Writer's Handbook

I.E: As an example let's use a FD seeking a new tanker truck. Here are the facts about the project:

They currently own a 1974 converted dairy/milk truck that holds 2000 gals of water.

It has no baffles in its tank so when you corner, the water sloshes around putting the truck off balance.

The weight of the water overworks the engine and brakes as it was not originally built to handle emergency responses where time is crucial.

The engine is under-powered and the braking system is faulty so as to have an ineffective response.

The community where you live is rural and there are no fire hydrants to draw water from so you have to carry water to each call you go on.

The truck no longer has parts available for it, so every time something breaks you have an extended period of downtime and parts must be custom manufactured for you to put the truck back in service.

Those parts are expensive and the truck is eating up your entire vehicle maintenance budget.

There are no safety belts in the truck and the electrical system is shorting out.

There are so many holes and pin hole leaks in the rusting tank that half the water load is leaked out by the time you get to a call and it has no pump to fill itself with, so you have to send a pumper with it to refill it every time.

What is the problem here for this department?

Is the problem that the truck needs replacement or that they need more hydrants? Actually, the problem is neither of those two statements but, many would mistakenly think so. In reality those statements actually describe the symptoms of a much larger problem for their department and community. Their actual problem is that they have an inadequate water supply with which to fight fires, which is keeping them from performing their basic mission.

*Program Approach/Project Description*

This section is designed to help you develop your approach, which is also referred to as the project design or activities section; so that the reviewer is clear as to how you plan to solve the problem. The program approach should outline exactly what you intend to do and tell the

## Step Three: The Grant Proposal

story in a chronological order. It is important to define your goal and tie in program activities connected with the problem. After reading this section, the reviewer should have no doubt as to what activities will take place and in what order. Remember that creating a new, innovative strategy will get the reader's attention and interest. Show how your program is "original." Sell your program!

---

In the last section you presented the problem and if you did a good job the reviewer believes that your community is in serious need of assistance. Now you will show them that you have a plan for lessening or resolving the problem. This section should clearly show how you will address the problem that you presented as well as point out the benefits of providing this program or assistance to your community. Make your explanations clear. Address a solution for each problem that you presented in the previous section. Show the reviewer that your plan can make a difference in your community.

Remember

---

### Gathering Information

☐ Begin by deciding on your purpose by asking yourself the following questions:

1. What is it that I want to accomplish?

Remember that you are trying to resolve or lessen the problem you presented in your Problem Statement.

2. Why am I developing this program?

3. What are my goals?

4. Does my purpose correspond with the RFP and is it aligned properly with the priorities of the funding source?

☐ Once you have decided on the purpose of your program, collect information to help transform your approach into innovative strategies. Consider these comments and questions.

1. Who knows a great deal about my purpose? Who is an expert on the topic I am pursuing? Have meetings and conduct interviews with these people to solicit information. They can suggest strategies and ideas you may have missed.

Networking is vitally important to initial and continued success at grant writing. This includes networking with fellow grant writers and also with experts you encounter in the various fields - past instructors of seminars you have attended, authors of books and training manuals you have read and used. Look for recognized individuals in your career field that have an intimate and recognized expertise in these areas and use this information to your advantage.

2. Do programs with similar purposes already exist? If so, talk with the people who were involved. You can also check the funder's website for model programs.

The Executive Summary which is included in many grants is the basis for putting forward Best Practices reports and ideas in a lot of grant programs.

3. Are there relevant studies and literature available?

Look for reports and data that will support your contentions. Go to websites and research reports from agencies that typically are identified as the country's leading authority on these types of problems like the FBI, National Criminal Justice Information System, The IAFC, IAPC, NFPA, USFA and others who have studied many of these issues already. Their reports contain a plethora of statistical data to support your contentions.

Look for statistics that will also back up your statements and then quote your statistics against the National levels. The Internet was the greatest boon to ever occur for grant writers. It saves countless hours of reading and trying to find these statistical databases and all of it can be accomplished through search engines with a few mouse clicks. Use that immensely powerful tool to your advantage. Others will not and this allows you to jump ahead of them in terms of presenting a comprehensive approach.

4. Obtain copies of grants with similar purposes that have been funded. They can provide valuable information, saving you time in the long run.

This is where having a professional grant consultant can be very critical for you.

Unfortunately, and especially in the first responder career fields, departments and other grant writers can be very protective of their grant work as they will look at you as competition. This is, of course, not helpful and sometimes makes it difficult to obtain funded examples.

Technically any grant application that has been funded by a Federal grant program is a matter of public record and as such would be subject to FOIA regulations but, nobody wants to go through that and form an adversarial relationship. NIMS dictates and mandates interagency cooperation and NIMS compliance is a first step requirement to getting funded by DHS. In that spirit, it is best to remember that the equipment you may be denying to your neighboring department by refusing to share your funded grant application with them may in fact someday be needed by them to bail you out of a real life or death situation. This deadly fact has been borne out to us in graphic detail on numerous occasions since helping departments and their mutual aid partners.

## Step Three: The Grant Proposal

---
5. Brainstorm with numerous people. Obtain different viewpoints. Ask the questions "what is the problem" and "how do we solve it?"

Tips

---

### Outlining Your Strategy

☐ Outlining your program is the first step in organizing your thoughts. Consider the following before outlining your strategy.

1. What program activities do I want to cover? Avoid talk of buying anything in this section unless your grant is seeking equipment only.

2. What does the RFP ask to be included? Once again this is a place where your comprehensive reading skills need to be put in gear. You should have already discerned what the funding source needs to see in order to fund you.

3. What are the main points?

4. What is the best way to organize this section for a clear picture of the program I am proposing?

Organizing it chronologically is the best way to start and it will assist you in writing a timeline which some grants may call for within the documents.

☐ Below is a basic outline of the major topics covered in a typical program approach. Begin by reviewing the outline below and then modify it to fit your program. Next, list key phrases and points you want to include. It is important to organize your thoughts in outline form before writing..

- Introduction (purpose)
- Target Population or Geographic Area
- Personnel Involved
- Program Activities
- Conclusion

### Writing The Program Approach

☐ Using the detailed outline you just created, begin writing your program approach. Remember to sell your program and include more details on each major topic.

☐ The introduction is the first paragraph of your program approach and acquaints the reviewer with it. Make this paragraph clear and concise with a quick overview.

www.HDGrants.com

Grant Writer's Handbook

1. Begin with the purpose or goal of the grant proposal. The purpose of (program name) is to... OR The goal of (program name) is to...

IE: The ABC FD is seeking funding to install 546 smoke detectors in the homes of our city to reduce the incidence of residential house fires by 12%.

2. Describe the target population in one sentence. This program will target... OR The focus of this program will be on...

IE: This program will be targeted at the identified high risk groups of elderly citizens over 65 years of age and youth that are 14 yoa and younger as per the program guidance.

3. Follow with a general overview of the specific activities that will occur in the grant. Components of this program will include... OR Program activities will consist of the following...

IE: components of this program will include identifying members of community that are within the targeted at risk groups, arranging for a team of our members to visit them and install the smoke detectors and perform a follow up visit in 6 months to replace the batteries in the smoke detectors once again.

4. Provide a transitional sentence that leads to the details of your program approach. The following information outlines the program in more detail... OR The activities below provide more information about (program name)...

☐ The next part of your program approach section should include a detailed description of the target population. Let the reviewer know exactly who will benefit from your program.

1. Who is the target population? You may have a primary target population and a secondary target population.

As an example the Fire Prevention and Safety grant, offered every year from FEMA, specifically states that the grant targets the "high risk group of elderly over the age of 65 and youths under the age of 14 years of age".

When addressing this, be sure that your program does not exclude one group by focusing strictly on the other. That would indicate that you are ignoring a group that the funding source sees as a priority and as such, you would be denied.

www.HDGrants.com

## Step Three: The Grant Proposal

2. Why were they selected?

The best reason to select a particular target group is because the RFP or program guidance stated that was a priority for them. There are usually clues hidden within the RFP that would identify who the grant proceeds need to benefit specifically. This may also be revealed simply in the name of the program such as a program entitled "Financial Exploitation of Elderly".

3. Where is the geographical area of the target population?

Sometimes grants are designated to serve specific populations in a specific geographical area such as specific census tracts. It might also be revealed to the grant writer through the title of the grant program such as a program from the Health and Rural Services Administration entitled " Increasing The Level Of Emergency Pediatric Care In Rural Communities"

4. How many people will be targeted?

This would be important information in allowing the funding source to determine the actual cost per person and subsequently gauge the "Bang for the Buck" or cost benefit of your project. This is a major factor for funding sources since they usually have only a limited amount of money and wish to see that money used to benefit the maximum number of people.

It also is used by DHS as a factor in determining the level of risk that exists. The logic here is that the greater the number of people in any given area, the higher the probability that some natural or manmade disaster would occur which required mitigation. Since they only have a limited amount of money to award, they will apportion that money or assign a greater need to those areas having greater populations concentrated in smaller areas.

It is extremely critical to have accurate population's counts that can be documented showing every man, woman and child which would benefit from the grant dollars being given to you. This is how you knock out the competition that fails to list such critical information.

5. Below is a list of possible other ways to identify your target population. Be sure to adequately describe the target population clearly.

- ☐ Number of participants
- ☐ Location of target population, such as city, neighborhood, park and geographical area.
- ☐ Use the adjectives that describes your group such as dealers, suspects and at-risk youth, etc

www.HDGrants.com

Grant Writer's Handbook

6. How will you identify your target population?

☐ A Task Force might be used to assist your program by providing recommendations, monitoring and evaluations.

- Reviewers usually like to see this in grants and may give you extra points for the effort. Answer these questions in your approach section.
- How many members will there be? What are their backgrounds?
- How are they selected?
- What are their responsibilities?

7. Reviewers also like to be assured that all stakeholders affected by the grant are represented, so steering committees are a good thing sometimes. You should ask yourself how will the committee be representative of all interested parties, especially with regards to culture, race, and gender.

8. Program activities should be spelled out in detail. The reviewer should know exactly what you intend to do and how you plan to solve or reduce the effects of your problem. Use your outline to keep your thoughts organized when writing your planned activities and consider these questions.

1. How will I show that my activities are strategies that will truly combat, prevent, and/or reduce the problems mentioned in the problem statement?

Do not forget that it is important here to show not only what activities you are going to do, but exactly why that activity is needed and what you hope to achieve.

Be sure to describe in sufficient detail what is going to take place. If you are going to teach a class then state how many times you will teach it, how many hours is it going to be, how many people are going to go through it, will they be tested and what is achieved by performing those activities.

What major activities do I want to cover?

What tasks do I need to perform or conduct that will show to the reviewer that our entire program will have an impact in the areas that the funding source seeks to serve. You have to form that nexus between the activity and the eventual accomplishment of the funding sources' goals.

What details do I need for each activity so that the reviewer is clear on what will take place?

## Step Three: The Grant Proposal

The proof of your program being comprehensive in scope, is in the details. This is what sets you apart from the competition. It shows the reviewer that you have in fact done your homework and have a well thought out plan of attack here.

- ☐ Who will be involved in each activity?
- ☐ Who, why and in what capacity
- ☐ What ways can I show that my activities are innovative and creative?
- ☐ What makes my program original and unique?
- ☐ Is it more efficient?
- ☐ Does it offer greater safety?
- ☐ Is it a new twist on an old way?
- ☐ What state or national models can I use to make my approach more valid?
- ☐ Can I cite a Best Practices award for something similar?
- ☐ Is this in line with or does it gain you compliance with some National standard that is well accepted?
- ☐ Is there scientific evidence from a report that you can quote that proves your point?
- ☐ What references, graphs, etc... can I use to show my activities are legitimate?
- ☐ Can I show that this was done elsewhere and that I can replicate those results here?

Be sure the application will allow you to use graphs or charts and that if using an eGrant application that there is a way for that to be submitted with the grant application.

How can I organize this section so that it is easy for the reviewer to follow? One effective way is to label subsections.

Most grant RFPs will specifically list what each section needs to speak to and that language may give you a clue as to the title header you should use and the order in which they should appear such as this language taken directly from the RFP/Program Guidance on the Fire Act grant for the SAFER program:

IE: "The narrative section of your grant should include information discussing the following":

**Project description:** This statement should describe what the applicant needs the grant funds for, i.e., how the newly-hired firefighters will be used within the department, and a description of the specific benefit these firefighters will provide for the fire department and

community. If the applicant is re-hiring laid-off firefighters, the narrative should explain when they were laid-off and how the layoffs have affected the service to the community.

**Impact on daily operations:** This statement should explain how the community and current firefighters are at risk without the requested firefighters, and to what extent that risk will be reduced if the applicant is awarded.

Financial need: This statement should explain the applicant's inability to address the need without Federal assistance.

**Minority recruitment:** This statement should describe the applicant's efforts to ensure, to the extent possible, that they will seek, recruit, and hire members of racial and ethnic minority groups and women to increase their ranks within the department.

**Financial obligation:** This statement should include plans to retain the new firefighter positions.

**Volunteer discrimination:** This statement should explain how the applicant plans to meet the requirement ensuring firefighters in positions filled under SAFER Grants are not discriminated against for, or prohibited from, engaging in volunteer activities in another department

The **bold** type indicates this is what they want you to use as the actual header titles within the narrative statement.

What training or consulting issues do I need to address?

Again this is an area where you are being checked as to the comprehensiveness of your application. Obviously if you were going for a communications project that was going to change frequencies or bands, then you would need to show the reviewer that you will have a consultant who has an Engineering degree in Radio Communications advising you on what you need to do or what type of equipment you will need in order to accomplish your goals. There are usually fees for providing those services and if you expect to pay for those fees with grant money, they would have to be justified within the narrative.

9. The conclusion gives an overview of what you have said in this section, reinforces the idea that your program approach is innovative, and will help prevent, reduce, or solve the problem. This paragraph should provide a wrap-up statement that leaves the reader on a positive note. Consider these comments and questions.

## Step Three: The Grant Proposal

1. In one or two sentences, how should I give a summary of my approach? You may want to mention the target population and the problem again by stating how it will be solved.

2. How can I leave the reviewer wanting to help?

3. How can I make the reviewer remember my program approach? Using the name of your program helps *especially in italics*.

4. IE: We have a major drug sales and gang violence problem in several of our residential neighborhoods at night. If the Lake Alfred PD's *"Operation Nightwatch"* program is granted funding, we can obtain the night vision devices needed to expose these criminals, removing the cloak of darkness which allows them to operate with impunity and which is causing the residents of these neighborhoods to cower in fear in their homes. With your assistance, and granting of our request, you will be instrumental in returning the safety and security of our neighborhood streets back to the citizens to whom it so rightfully belongs.

### Program Approach Section Checklist

The following are ideas and suggestions to consider in your approach section.

- ☐ 1. This section begins with the purpose or goal of the grant proposal followed by specific activities that will occur in the grant.
- ☐ 2. The approach section should not be wordy, but relate specific detailed information.
- ☐ 3. The approach tells a story and discusses the activities in a chronological order.
- ☐ 4. The approach flows well, linking each paragraph to one another (use connecting words such as next, also, additionally, first, second, in conclusion and use connecting sentences such as "the following outlines the program in more detail.").
- ☐ 5. The writer should avoid repeating the same word or phrases too many times.
- ☐ 6. Avoid the use of negative terms such as "Officers will be required to..."
- ☐ 7. The approach section should be written in a positive tense, as if the writer "will" obtain the grant.
- ☐ 8. Stay program oriented and avoid talking about simply buying things. Your concern should be focused on what occurs after you have these tools or equipment and the results that will be achieved.
- ☐ 9. The approach has a catchy, but relevant, title in italics.
- ☐ 10. The target population is described clearly, with the number of participants and the reasons that they were selected.
- ☐ 11. Numbers are spelled out in this section. IE: one, two, three… not 1,2,3
- ☐ 12. Tell why each activity is important and who will be involved in each activity.

# Grant Writer's Handbook

- ☐ 13. Avoid the usage of complex words or phrases that are difficult to understand, and stay away from slang or shop talk. Keep your target reading audience in mind.
- ☐ 14. Try to avoid acronyms all together. If you must use them, be sure to spell them out first at least once per page.
- ☐ 15. Keep your proposed activities interesting, appealing, and unique.
- ☐ 16. Include graphics, graphs, and charts (if space and the RFP allows).
- ☐ 17. Include state or national program models in the discussion.
- ☐ 18. For each problem discussed, make sure there is a corresponding strategy stated that accompanies it.
- ☐ 19. Mention the program frequently.
- ☐ 20. Provide a brief wrap-up that leaves the reader with a good feeling. And do not forget to thank the reviewers for their time and efforts on your behalf.

## Financial Need

Remember — Let's make something clear right up front here. The mere lack of an adequate operating budget, in and of itself, is not sufficient reason to establish financial need in a grant. I mean, after all, most departments do not apply for the grant because they are flush with money; that's a given fact.

Almost all grants are awarded because there is a strong financial need for assistance. There exists a gap between a problem that exists and the financial resources needed to resolve that problem; the grant should seek to fill that gap. This is one of the primary reasons that grants exist and it is therefore reasonable to expect that a funding source will require a strong statement of financial need prior to approving any application for funding.

Must Do — Key Point #5 - Failing to provide a strong statement of financial need is one of the most common reasons that grants are rejected. In this area of your grant, you should work diligently to make a very compelling statement, it will account for as much as 25% of your total grant score.

You must always keep in mind who it is that will be reading your grant; remember there will usually be 3-5 people reading it and you must account for the idiosyncrasies of each of them. Some people are swayed or influenced by words and some rationalize their decision by mathematical calculation; left side–right side of the brain thinkers. Just as in your daily life there will likely be at least one person in that group who would be labeled as a "number cruncher"; they like math and are good at it. They need things spelled out in terms of the "bottom line" and if they do not see the information that they need to rationalize their decision in their heads, they will move on to an application that does give them that information. It is almost as if psychologically they will be saying to themselves, "I cannot

## Step Three: The Grant Proposal

make a decision about whether someone is financially needy, unless I see their budget". You must remember that if that person happens to be the swing vote on the panel in reaching a majority decision that is favorable to you and you fail to provide what they need in terms of financial information to justify that, you lose that vote. That one vote may be the difference between "awarded or denied".

You should always begin the financial needs section by explaining your current budget and where that budget comes from. The reviewer will want to see that you have a set budget amount, that it is relatively stable and that, frankly, it just isn't enough to enable you to do what needs to be done.

Again this goes to the psychology involved with the human minds reading your budget information. Fail to provide that detailed information and you run the risk of losing that 25 points you need here to gain an award. If you simply jump out there and say that "the operational budget of my department is $2.5 million dollars per year," this is going to hit some reviewers badly. Consider that the person reading this may be from a small rural agency with only 3 officers in it and they operate on less than $250,000 a year. Their initial reaction, after reading such a statement as that, could very well be "Wow, this department is not financially needy, they have 10 times more budget per year than I do".

You have to put that $2.5 million into proper perspective for them by showing exactly where that money is going. You must force them to rate or compare your financial need in an "apples to apples" comparison and not use an "apples to oranges" comparison to themselves. You allow them to do that by providing sufficient detail so that their mathematically oriented minds can see a bottom line and clearly draw a conclusion that when you have legitimate expenditures yearly that use up all of your available budget, little is left over to purchase the items you are seeking from the grant program and, thereby, proving that you are financially needy.

Simply saying that salaries and benefits use 87% of your budget is meaningless unless they know what your actual budget is to begin with. You have to give the reviewer perspective here and quantify things so that they can make a fair comparison to others.

You need to have some basic information before you begin this section, so let us look at some of the things you will need and start this section by answering a few questions:

- ☐ What was your budget for the last year?
- ☐ Where did it come from?
- ☐ How much did you raise in private fundraising?

www.HDGrants.com                                                                                              101

Grant Writer's Handbook

☐ Do you have other grant program monies working in that budget?

☐ What investment or "rainy day" funds have you set aside?

☐ Is there a capital improvements fund?

☐ Has the budget been stable for at least three years?

Now you need to explain to the reviewer what you do with your operational budget. Many reviewers are "number crunchers" and one of the first things they will scan for on your applications is what your financial condition is or what you have available from local financial resources. Make this section easy for the reviewer. Draw up a simple table with columns for expenditures vs. income. Be sure to show the reviewers what you expend for the following, and list these costs under the accompanying headings.

Income:
☐ Tax-based income
☐ Investment income
☐ Fundraising
☐ Grants
☐ Donations received
☐ Total budget

Expenditures or Expenses:
☐ Salaries and benefits
☐ Workman's compensation insurance
☐ Vehicle insurance
☐ Utilities
☐ Vehicle maintenance
☐ Fuel
☐ Mortgage payments
☐ Debt service
☐ Equipment
☐ Training

After delineating the above items you must show what is impacting your budget. This is where you define the problem that you are trying to deal with. It is perfectly acceptable to

## Step Three: The Grant Proposal

admit that your department isn't populated with financial wizards. What they are looking for here is to see effort on your part to resolve your own financial problems.

The reviewer is not in your town, so you'll need to accurately describe what it is like in your area economically and why you are having problems. What socio-economic conditions are affecting the ability of the citizens to support the department? This is commonly referred to as demographics.

---

Much of the demographics about your area can be obtained at the American Fact Finder website maintained by the US Census Bureau. A fact sheet regarding your area can be obtained by city name, county, or zip code. That site is located at: (http://factfinder.census.gov/home/saff/main.htm)

Tips

---

This fact sheet, from American Fact Finder, gives you statistical information about the area requested and compares it to National averages:

Average median income levels

Average median home values

Number of disabled or senior citizens living on fixed incomes

Poverty levels

Educational levels

This information can be used to your advantage in trying to provide a true and accurate representation of what it is like economically in your area.

Some of the information that would be of interest to the reviewer would be:

☐ How successful have you been at private fundraising?

☐ Many of you will have local policies which prohibit private fundraising, and you need to let the reviewer know this. Typically law enforcement agencies do not allow soliciting for supplemental funding from businesses locally which is OK except that you should tell the reviewer that the practice is prohibited via charter or SOPs from within the department. However, fire and other first responder organizations usually do not have such prohibitions in place and the funding source will wish to see what effort is being made locally to resolve these financial issues.

☐ Nobody is going to expect you to conduct 300 boot drives to raise $250,000 to purchase the new fire engine but, they do have a valid expectation that you are making an effort to handle your financial needs from within available methods.

www.HDGrants.com

Grant Writer's Handbook

☐ Any disasters that have affected the donations from local businesses and citizens (hurricanes, tornadoes, floods, etc.) Natural and manmade disasters usually have a long term effect that is felt for years in recovering from these events. Typically cities are self insured and the uninsured losses that occur from a catastrophic natural disaster can have a negative impact upon available local financial resources for up to 10 years in some cases. There is also a ripple effect here in the local community as businesses and citizens will also be impacted severely and this inhibits their likelihood to have supplemental discretionary financial resources that they can contribute.

☐ Have you had any major economic catastrophes that have, or are going to, impact your budget for a considerable period of time?

☐ Did the local factory close its doors or move their operations to foreign locations in search for cheaper labor?

☐ Has a drought impacted the local agricultural crop forecasts or harvests? If the local economy is driven by agricultural interests, this can have a devastating effect on the local economy. It should also be remembered that local economies which are agriculturally based are impacted drastically by fuel prices and tax value of land for agricultural purposes are usually significantly lower than values for residential or commercial based property. That can affect the tax base from which public safety agency budgets are usually drawn upon.

☐ Was a new law passed such as a "Spotted Owl" endangered species act that shut down the local logging industry, or did changes occur in "commercial fishing" regulations? Environmental activism has been responsible in some areas for turning economically viable towns into virtual ghost towns, when some of these laws were passed. The timber and mining industries in some areas have been virtually eliminated, not from a lack of resources but simply because the industry was regulated out of business

---

**Remember:** Did you actually ask for the items in your annual budget request, and it was shot down? It is certainly reasonable on the part of a funding source to wonder if you have attempted to get your local governing boards to fund your needs. The reason you are seeking grant support should be driven because local financial resources are tapped out and unavailable to you now or in the immediate foreseeable future.

---

☐ Did they give you a reason why? It is acceptable that budget requests get turned down. It happens all across the country every year. After all the financial resources available do have limits but, they will want to know why the request was turned down. Other needs within areas take away from what resources are available to supplement your budget. Maybe a new school had to be built or the city is facing fines from the EPA because they must dig new water wells to eliminate PCBs in their well water. Be sure

104      www.HDGrants.com

## Step Three: The Grant Proposal

that you are giving the reviewer sufficient information so that they can clearly see why your governing board would refuse your request.

- ☐ Did a line item in your budget get hit by a swing of the budget axe? This is a common occurrence and is happening more and more frequently in the current financial crisis being faced across the country. Administrators are being asked to "look for fat" or cut non-essential services and expenditures as local financial economies are faced with decreased tax based funding. Capital improvement budgets typically are one of the first things that get cut and projects are indefinitely put on hold as those garnered resources are tapped to provide operational capital to maintain continuity of operations.

- ☐ Was a local tax referendum proposed? Nobody likes to see a tax increase, even we as public safety employees are impacted by such decisions but here again, the reviewers want to know that an attempt was made to secure this funding through local efforts even though those efforts may have been futile.

- ☐ Were the local politicians afraid to put it on the ballot for fear of voter reaction? This is a huge factor especially if it happens to be an election year. It is generally considered to be political suicide for a politician to propose a tax increase of any sort while also seeking election or re-election to office.

- ☐ Did the voters actually vote it down? Hey, it happens! You put together what logically makes sense on paper, is relatively small in personal financial impact, it is put on the ballot for approval and it gets shot down by the voters. It happens every day even though the public in most cases has no true concept of the long term effects of voting these issues down. Remember that we operate in a career field in public safety that is largely not in the daily forefront of people's minds. They expect the services to be there but are relatively unaware of the true costs associated with providing such services. The old adage of "nobody thinks about the fire department until their own house is on fire" has a lot of validity here.

- ☐ Has there been gross financial mismanagement by previous administrations?
  - This is really quite common, especially in very small towns.
  - It is acceptable to admit this has occurred in your own town, provided that definitive corrective action has been implemented and steps have been put in place to prevent it from occurring again. Reviewers will also wish to know if prosecutorial efforts were or are being pursued.
  - Has there been a criminal act committed against your department that you have had to deal with?
  - Did a city or department employee embezzle money?

- Did someone commit arson to your station house or vehicles?
- Was a squad car or ambulance stolen and then trashed or burned?
- ☐ Were any actions taken at your State level that affected your bottom line in tax revenues being collected or distributed?
  - Was a "Proposition 13" or similar type bill passed by your legislature limiting the ability of local authorities to raise taxes or that placed a cap on what can be asked for in any one given year?
  - Has the State discovered that there is a severe budget deficit and they have withheld expected sales tax revenue?
  - Was a "balanced budget" amendment passed by the voters and the State is required to deal with this, causing tax revenue shortfalls?
- ☐ Have there been other major financial needs that local officials have had to take action on, causing you to have budget shortfalls?
  - A new water plant had to be built?
  - Road construction project has taken precedence and received a large chunk of your local available tax dollars.
  - Public school initiatives are being addressed.
- ☐ Did you have a major failure in another department that needed to be taken care of?
- ☐ Were you previously turned down for a grant and had to use your budget for that?
- ☐ Have you incurred significant debt service for the next 10 years?
- ☐ Did you just build a new station?

Finally, you need to address the consequences to your department and budget if you are not granted the award. How would rejection of this grant request impact your future operating budget? What will have to be put off in order to deal with this issue? How many years will it take you to raise the money on your own?

Adequately addressing your financial need should be accomplished in no less than three paragraphs. I have seen grants where financial need was referred to in one sentence. This is entirely too little, and the grant would never be funded since the grant program is predicated upon the "financial needs" of the department that it is meant to serve.

On the next pages we have provided you with several examples of compelling financial needs' statements from DHS grants that were funded.

## Step Three: The Grant Proposal

### Sample of Financial Need

#### Financial Need:

The majority of our budget is dedicated to personnel costs (75%) with the remaining going toward equipment, operating and maintenance costs. We are expecting a budget shortfall due to the increasing price of fuel and are expecting the city to have to dip into emergency fund to pay for the fuel cost throughout the city departments, with some departments having to cut back on services. In 2003 the only aerial apparatus we had suffered a complete hydraulic failure and had to be replaced with a new aerial at a cost of $???????? This has forced the city to cut back all of our expenses and place the truck on a 10 year plan in order to finance it at an annual debt service payment of $???????. This has left our equipment fund at only $8,250 per year.

We are located in the middle of Appalachia, historically one of the most impoverished areas in the United States. According to the Census Bureau 2000 report, a full 30.5% of our citizens live below the poverty level. The average median household income is only $20,690, which is 49% below the U.S. average of $41,994. The median value of a home in our area is only $74,800, which is 63% below the U.S. established level of $119,600. The largest employer in our region, Appalachian Regional Health Care has a union strike in progress, with no agreement in site. DJ Nypro a plastic injection molding company has closed a factory that sits just a few hundred feet from our fire station number 2 and moved those 125 jobs to a different area. Sykes, a computer call center located in the industrial park has closed and transferred operations to India laying off 750 workers. Trus Joist, a division of Weyerhaeuser, had laid off all but 100 of their employees indefinitely. The downsizing and impending closing of Trus Joist and the closing of Sykes has eliminated the two largest companies in our industrial park and has removed a significant share of tax based revenues as a result and created an economic crisis in this area for our residents, as they scramble to find new employment.

The coal industry has slowed significantly due to EPA regulations, global warming/greenhouse gases concerns and the conversion of most electrical generation plants to natural gas and is now expecting a recession thus mandating further layoffs and additional downsizing as well. This will almost certainly exclude the possibility of tax increases for our existing population.

The State of Kentucky as well as local organizations are recruiting additional industry to our region, but must offer wide spread tax break incentive packages to get them to move here. The area has also seen several of these businesses close and relocate as soon as the incentives run out. It is hoped that the current commercial and residential growth that we are experiencing will at least pay for the additional demands being placed on our department. We have seen a growth in our run volume of approximately 40% from 2003 to 2005, and this is with the reduction of the number of emergency medical calls. We had previously always dispatched a rescue unit on all medical calls, but were forced to cut back to only running calls that the dispatch center deemed as emergency ALS. We have had dramatic increases in the number of auto accidents as well as increases in the number of automatic aid and mutual aid calls for rescue tools and manpower.

FY 06 Budget

Income:

Taxes $1,050,800

Fundraisers $3000

Grant Writer's Handbook

Donations $1,500

State Aid $8,250.00

TOTAL INCOME $1,063,550

Expenses:

Salaries and Benefits $750,700

Professional Technical Services $12,000

Apparatus Payments $134,500

Uniform Clothing $46,900

Training and Related Travel $4,500

Building Maintenance $10,000

Radio Tower Rental $1,200

Technical Supplies $25,500

Office Supplies $4,500

Fuel $8,500

Utilities $11,400

Vehicle Maintenance $17,000

Dues & Subscriptions $100

Insurance & Bonds $23,000

Technical Equipment $1,000

Equipment $8,250

Fire Prevention $4,500

TOTAL EXPENSES $1,063,550

We have invested significant time and effort in our personnel to have them properly trained to provide for the needs of our area in emergency services and rescue work. We are the go-to resource for our entire county as far as heavy rescue work is concerned. Unfortunately we find ourselves in the unenviable position of having the trained technicians to do the job, but lacking the proper tools to do their tasks. We are without the financial resources to properly equip these members to perform these vitally needed functions and lives are being lost as a result. Outside financial assistance is needed to bridge this expanding gap in our services.

## Cost Benefit

In this section, you want to explain the benefit of funding you. This, like many other sections you will find in this book, may or may not be required under the guidelines or RFP.

## Step Three: The Grant Proposal

Regardless of whether it is a required section or not, you should still include some wording to prove cost benefit.

---

Cost benefit is about "saving money". Cost benefit should state the benefits of the funding to your department, to your mutual aid partners and to the community you serve. We call that addressing the "triumvirate" of us, we and them.. Describe for the reviewer how or why this problem is costing each of those groups money. Then explain in detail how, when you receive this equipment or funding, each group will benefit.

Remember

---

Another way to think of cost benefit is to consider it as "Bang for the Buck". It is taking an item that you are obtaining with grant funding and spreading the monetary value of that item across a large group of people. The more people who can benefit the better.

Let's examine the cost benefit to all three of the above groups associated with receiving a grant award to obtain new turnout gear for a group of volunteer firefighters.

The department itself receives cost benefit by protecting its people from getting injured and this saves money for the department by:

- ☐ Reducing the uninsured medical costs associated with deductibles at emergency rooms and hospitals
- ☐ It stabilizes or reduces the premiums being paid by the department for Workman's Compensation
- ☐ It reduces the chance of liability from lawsuit should a firefighter be injured or killed in the line of duty
- ☐ Overtime is saved if an injury is prevented and someone does not have to take that injured firefighter's place while he or she recovers
- ☐ It prevents spending money to retrain a new firefighter to take the place of on who has been permanently disabled or killed
- ☐ The chance that firefighter's will leave your department and migrate to another department that offers safer equipment is reduced
- ☐ The department assures itself that all personnel are properly equipped to perform the tasks that they are assigned safely
- ☐ Money set aside to handle other critical needs within the department does not have to be diverted to purchase this basic necessity

In the case of volunteer firefighters, their families place less pressure on them to stop volunteering for you if they know that the firefighter is properly equipped and will return

www.HDGrants.com
109

Grant Writer's Handbook

safely to them at the end the end of the call which prevents additional money being spent to recruit, train and equip new firefighters

How does your members having proper and safe turnout gear save money for your mutual aid partners?

- ☐ When the other department encounters a situation where they have a temporary need to supplement their own manpower, your people are properly equipped to go to that call and be of true value to them. If your members show up in ragged equipment they cannot be committed to the task that needs to be done safely for fear of liability to the other department should they be hurt. In essence, if not properly equipped, they become nothing but another "rubbernecker" standing idly by and are useless to the mutual aid department.
- ☐ By knowing that your members are properly equipped it saves money for the mutual aid department in not being required to recruit, train and equip additional members for themselves to cover temporary manpower shortages that they occasionally experience.
- ☐ All of the reasons listed above for saving money for your own department are also applicable to the mutual aid department as well for the very same reasons that it saves your department money.

Lastly, how does you department members having new safe turnout gear save money for your citizens that they are sworn to protect, not just in their own areas of responsibility but also the citizens in the extended mutual aid community as well?

A properly equipped firefighter is less likely to hesitate to commit to an interior attack or Search and Rescue mission if they have confidence in their own equipment to adequately protect them while performing such tasks. A quicker response without hesitation leads to a reduction in the actual property damage losses or loss of life occurring during these calls.

- ☐ Having properly equipped firefighters and keeping those dollar losses and loss of life form occurring offers cost benefit by stabilizing or actually lowering the ISO rating of a community. This results in the property owner paying lees in premiums to their home owners insurance company.
- ☐ It can prevent taxes from being raised to cover the costs of purchasing this crucial equipment for the fire department
- ☐ Proper search and rescue, in the initial stages of a residential or commercial business fire, can result in lives being saved. If a citizen dies in a fire there is an economic ripple effect caused in the community. A taxpayer is lost and income that would be spent by that citizen is no longer being spent in the community. Widows and orphans move

## Step Three: The Grant Proposal

from your community depriving your area of further tax based income and or they go on welfare further burdening the welfare system of your area.

These are just some of the area that "cost savings" are realized for the department, the mutual aid departments and the citizens. These principles above can be applied to any equipment that might be obtained through a grant by a department if you think in terms of "money being saved".

---

Do not confuse "Cost Benefit" with "Operational Outcomes". The Cost Benefit section is about "saving money"; it is not about how it will "allow your department morale to improve" or "be able to better serve the public".

No No

---

All grant programs are usually inundated with applications and the amount of money available to be awarded is always far less than the money being requested. As an example the 2009 Assistance to Firefighters Grant Program received in excess of 22K applications yet traditionally only 5K awards will be made from this pool of grant money. By the rules of the AFG program only 25%, of the total money available in the program can be awarded to purchase firefighting apparatus/vehicles. In last year's program that meant only about 750 new trucks would be awarded with the $141 million dollars available yet the program received over $2 billion dollars in requests for new vehicles. The competition is intense and logistically this creates a nightmare for the program office to deal with.

Think about that for a minute.. 22K applications of 12-15 pages each would have to be read and scored and this administrative process would not only take an enormous amount of time, but would quickly deplete all of the money available in the program and there would not be any money left to actually award out in the grants. As such there must be a way to determine which applications are the most likely to meet the goals of the program and which express the strongest need for assistance. Resultantly, cost benefit is one of the things that is scored to determine the "competiveness" of a grant application.

---

This is usually accomplished via a computer which means that there are mathematical equations which are analyzed to determine competitive range scoring. Should your grant fail to make it past this competitive scoring, then it means that a human being on a reviewing panel never reads your grant. If you lose the scoring process at this point, all of your work to put together a decent and informative narrative for you application is for naught.

Remember

---

In both the competitive scoring (done by a computer) and in the review panel (where you can always count on a "bean counter" being present on the panel) an examination of the cost benefit will occur. The "cost benefit" can most easily be expressed by a mathematical formula.

www.HDGrants.com

111

Grant Writer's Handbook

Now the computer will already have the analog based formula and will compute it based upon answers that you put into boxes provided in sections of the application but, for the benefit of the reviewer reading and trying to place a subjective score on your grant, it is most easily expressed through a mathematical formula.

Let's examine cost benefit per person and how it is figured. Every piece of equipment that you would obtain is assigned a service life. This is determined by either:

The recommendation of certifying bodies such as the NIJ or NFPA. For instance a bullet proof vests service life is 5 years according to recommendations of the National Institute of Justice ( NIJ), which is an accepted interpretation. The National Fire Protection Association (NFPA) has similar type recommendations for equipment for fire departments. Most grant program applications would be geared towards those standards if they exist for equipment you are seeking to replace.

It can also be based on the equipment replacement cycle you have historically used. In other words if your agency buys a new fire truck every 25 years on average, then that standard would be acceptable. If they replace a squad car every 5 years then that might also be acceptable.

For our purposes of demonstrating these mathematical formulas, we will use as an example, a fire department seeking to replace their SCBA ( Self Contained Breathing Apparatus).

The known mathematical values needed for these calculations are as follows:

Population of primary response area = 5,000

Population of the mutual aid areas covered = 15,000

Cost of project 20 - SCBAs at $5,000 each or total project cost = $100,000

Annual average call volume that SCBA is used on = 500 calls per year

Service life of SCBA = 10 years

In order to figure the cost benefit of the project, on a cost per person basis, the following calculation is done:

Population of primary response area X service life of equipment = total persons served by the grant funding over the life of equipment. In this case:

5,000 X 10 = 50,000 persons served

## Step Three: The Grant Proposal

You would then divide that figure into the total project cost or:

50,000 divided into $100,000 = $2.00 cost per person

Now generally speaking good cost benefit is obtained if the cost per person is under $1.00 per person. Obviously here in this example we did not achieve that but, if we now add the fact that you also use SCBA when you go to answer a mutual aid call, then we can add the 15,000 additional population of those areas into those formulas. In doing so, we can further reduce the cost benefit per person to the following:

Mutual aid population + primary response population X service life of equipment

20,000 population X  10 = 200,000 people served.

200,000 divided into $100,000 = $ .50 per person… a much better cost per person to put forward to a reviewer.

The other factor figured in cost benefit is the frequency of use which is normally calculated for items over $50K in cost. That formula is:

Average calls per year equipment is used X service life of equipment = Total calls equipment will be used in its lifetime. In the above stated situation that would be:

500 calls per year average X 10 years  = 5000 calls the SCBA would be used in their service life

5000 calls divided into $100,000 = $20 per call and when extrapolated across 20 sets of SCBA would yield a cost per call / per unit of $1.00 per call as frequency of use.

That means that every time a call is answered it is costing the grant program $1.00 per SCBA to answer that call.

The cost benefit of a project when calculated by the computer for purposes of "competitive range" scoring will not usually consider your mutual aid population and is based only on the permanent population of your area. Populations that temporarily fluctuate daily, or seasonally, will not be counted by the computer when scoring. These are called "transient populations" and include categories of person such as:

☐ Daily office workers flooding a business or office/skyscraper complex district

☐ College and University student populations

☐ Tourist populations

☐ Large theme park populations

www.HDGrants.com

113

☐ State prison populations

Now obviously these populations do in fact contribute to our call runs daily but, we will show you how to utilize them shortly.

Since you are only allowed to use the permanent resident population of your primary response area it is easy to see that some projects can quickly exceed the recommended levels to obtain a decent cost per person ratio and unfortunately that figure, if too high, can result in being scored as non-competitive. This would generate the reviled "Dear John" or rejection notice on your application.

In examining the above formulas you can see that you have no influence or ability to change your call volume or your population. The numbers are what the numbers are! There is only one number that you can change and that is the "total cost " of the project.

You must bear in mind that the goal of all funding sources who give out money each year is to extend help to as many departments as they can given the available funding that they have to award. For that reason, cost benefit is a critical area of concern in scoring a grant application. The only way to "beat big blue" at this point is to lower the cost of the project you are seeking which means you will have to offer up more of your own money towards that project. The recent ARRA stimulus package awards for Fire Station Construction were a prime example of this when the RFP for the programs contained language such as " higher consideration will be given to those projects that offer a substantial investment of their own matching dollars".

A grant writer needs to be careful in this area as you can very easily shoot yourself in the foot and destroy your financial need by offering to give too much of your own money. Think about if in this way.

If you go into a bank seeking a mortgage for a house and you offer up 25% or more of the total cost of the home, the bank will welcome you with open arms as a "good candidate" for a mortgage. The less you offer to contribute, the less likely you are to get a decent interest rate or even a loan at all. The reason you are seeking grant assistance should be that you have exhausted all other means of obtaining the money to finance your purchase, including the ability to borrow the money from a commercial loan source.

If you find that your cost benefit is too high and likely to be rejected by the computer, then you need to consider adding more of your own money to the pot to lower the initial purchase cost that the computer is basing its decision on. Let's work this out in a hypothetical scenario using a $200,000 dollar fire truck purchase as an example.

## Step Three: The Grant Proposal

Cost of truck = $200,000

Permanent population = 5,000 residents

Average call volume = 300 runs per year

Service life of truck = 25 years

Cost benefit on a cost per person ratio would calculate at:

5,000 pop X 25 years = 125,000 residents served during service life of truck

125,000 divided into the cost of $200,000 = $1.60 per person over life of truck

The frequency of use would calculate at :

300 calls per year average X 25 years = 7500 calls the truck would be used on.

7500 divided into $200,000 = $26.66 per call on frequency of use

Now let's change these dynamics slightly. The grant program will require you to put 5% local matching dollars with the grant so we want to reduce the cost of the truck by 20%. We would take the 15% additional money and apply that against the price of the true purchase price of the truck. This would reduce the cost of the truck by $30,000 to only $170,000. Now lets refigure that cost per person and frequency of use using those figures.

125,000 population divided into $170,000 = $1.36 per person cost benefit ratio

7500 divided into $170,000 = $22.66 per call for frequency of use

These might not seem like really big changes but when factored over the service life of the truck, they can make a significant difference in the scoring. The goal here is to get your application into the competitive range so a human being will be forced to read it. At that point we can now utilize a little psychological trick.

The human mind tends to remember the last figure that it reads so this is where we are going to bring in your mutual aid population figures or your transient population figures. The idea here is to "plant a seed" in the reviewers mind. A piece of information, once read, is retained, even if subliminally in the readers mind.

I am sure you have all seen a court TV show, or an actual trial, where a prosecuting attorney solicits a response to a question from a witness and the defense attorney jumps to their feet and screams, "I object, that is irrelevant or not admissible" and the judge rules in the defense attorney's favor and issues a verbal instruction to the jury that they will "disregard the last statement of the witness". In most cases the prosecuting attorney knew it would be

inadmissible and did this on purpose because, regardless of the instruction of the judge, the statement is heard and will probably be one of the statements that the jury remembers above all. The "trigger has been pulled" you cannot recall the bullet or the "bell as been rung" and you cannot un-ring it.

We need to make use of that little trick here also. You would do that by not only stating what the cost benefit formulas are using your permanent resident population but then, by immediately adding language to include your mutual aid or transient population showing how much lower the cost benefit becomes. We want that statement to be the last figure the reviewer reads. As an example let's use the above scenario but now add a mutual aid population of 10,000 more persons and an additional 53 calls per year in run call volume for mutual aid. The figures would now change to:

>Permanent population 5,000 + 10,000 mutual aid population = Total population served of 15,000 per year
>
>15,000 population X 25 years service life = 375,000 total person served
>
>$170,000 divided by 375,000 persons = $0.45 cents per person cost benefit

Frequency of use changes by:

>300 calls in primary response area + 53 calls to mutual aid area + 353 calls per year the truck will answer
>
>353 X 25 years = 8,825 calls the truck will answer in its lifetime.
>
>$170,000 divided by 8825 calls = $19.26 cents per call frequency of use

These are significant factors in lowering that cost and offering cost benefit. It also allows another significant factor to come into play here.

Remember what the goal of the reviewers is to start with, award as many departments as possible with the funding they have available to award. Well, if you offer to allow them to supply a $200,000 truck for the cost of only $170,000 they save $30,000. Now, if you were buying a truck on your own and a dealer offered it to you for $170,000 while the dealer across the street was selling it for $200,000, who would you buy from? You would opt to save yourself $30,000. That is exactly what you are doing. The reviewer in this case is a buyer seeking to buy a truck and looking for the best deal offered.

If you extend this on out using a reviewer's mind set, if he saves $30K with you and then does that with 7 other applicants, what has occurred? They have now saved enough money to

## Step Three: The Grant Proposal

fund another truck for another department. You might be thinking this is great in theory but, where is the proof that this works?

In an average year on the Assistance to Firefighters Grant Program we will file 400-500 applications for various Fire and EMS agencies across the U.S. for both Operations & Safety and Vehicle Acquisitions combined. During the years of 2004-2006 we simply allowed the applicant agencies to put in only the 5% or 10% that they were required to do and we would win about 16-18 trucks for these agencies in an average year. That was a pretty good average considering how many agencies applied for vehicles each year. Since 2006 we have applied the techniques related above. In year 2007 AFG our clients won 46 vehicles, in 2008 they won 51 vehicles. This is a significant finding and proof that the theory does produce significantly more awards.

Tips

I.E.: Here is a cost benefit statement utilizing the above referenced techniques

*We feel that the most important reason to apply for funding to purchase this tanker is for the safety of our firefighters, our community, and the interoperability with our mutual aid departments. However, everyone involved will realize the cost benefit of replacing this tanker. Many of our members cannot physically operate the existing tanker and they all fear for their safety in doing so. These concerns are valid and present a liability issue for our department. By replacing this tanker, we will reduce the amount of funding necessary to continue to make the untimely repairs that face us annually. As its condition continues to deteriorate, these repairs will increase in frequency and costs are sure to escalate. We are also exploring the possibility of removing the 1978 pumper/rescue from service, if funding for this tanker is secured. If we are able to follow through with this plan, removing two high maintenance vehicles from service will have an even greater cost benefit to our department.*

*We have debated about immediately removing this tanker from service, but this will drastically reduce the amount of available water for our initial attack. If removed, property loss will rise and the danger of possible lives lost both to our firefighters and our citizens will increase. This will have an effect on our community's insurance rates as our ISO rating is surely going to deteriorate. The cost of the average resident's fire insurance could increase as much as 50% because of this rating. By replacing our tanker, this ISO rating will be preserved with the possibility of it improving. By this happening, a financial savings for our residents will occur.*

*The replacement of this tanker will also have a cost benefit to our mutual aid partners by providing them with a critical resource. The reliability of this tanker to arrive in a timely manner will improve their fire suppression capabilities. It will also increase our interoperability with these departments as the need for additional resources at a fill site will not be as necessary. This will reduce the costs of operations and free up the manpower necessary to fill this unit, diverting them instead to where they are most needed- fighting the fire.*

*As can be seen with the age of our current fleet, vehicles within our department have an estimated lifespan of 25 years. The cost benefit of purchasing this tanker for our primary response area alone is $1.80 per person*

www.HDGrants.com

### Grant Writer's Handbook

per year. This is calculated by taking the cost of the vehicle ($293,000) and dividing it by the population (6511) resulting in the cost per year. To complete this cost benefit, this value is then divided by the lifespan of the vehicle (25 years). When one takes into consideration the areas covered with our mutual aid departments this past year, the coverage population increases to 30,809 residents. Calculating this additional cost benefit, take the cost of vehicle (293000) / total population of our first due/mutual aid area (30809). Then divide this result by the lifespan (25 years). The cost benefit decreases dramatically to $.38 per person per year.

Additional cost benefit has been provided by our department in this application in the following manner. The actual cost of this vehicle is $345,740. Through our departments fund raising efforts and policies of frugal fiduciary management, we have been able to accrue an additional $52,740 (18%) that we are committing towards the cost of this project in addition to the 5% required matching local share. Awarding this truck to our department will deliver a $345,750 new pumper for the cost of only $293,000. It is hoped that the additional overmatching dollars contributed by our department, and the savings this affords the AFG program, will allow the reviewers sufficient funding that can be combined such to award another less fortunate department to acquire a badly needed firefighting vehicle.

These are additional actual Cost Benefit sections from first round approved AFGP grants.

### Cost Benefit From AFGP Grant Proposal

*"Our department is comprised of all volunteer firefighters. Most of us are multi-generational, long-term residents born and raised in this community. The lives and homes of their immediate families and their sense of responsibility to their neighbors are the principal reasons for their dedication and participation in the Volunteer Fire Department."*

*"We rely on the continued service of these volunteers to sustain the high level of service that our community has become accustomed to. In order for us to encourage new volunteers, and account for aging volunteers, we need to assure that our volunteers can perform this vitally needed community service safely and still return home safely to their families and jobs after the call is over. Recruitment and training of new members is costly to us and we are already operating with limited financial resources. Their safety is compromised and the volunteers are beginning to become increasingly frustrated that they are forced to function under adverse and dangerous conditions without benefit of proper SCBA equipment. Obtaining this equipment will serve as a retention and recruitment tool to help us maintain our current membership."*

*"The FFs are losing confidence in the aged equipment we are currently using. This causes them to hesitate to commit to an initial attack as they check and re-check this equipment to be certain that they have a full functioning air pack. As a result, we are suffering fire damage property losses for our residents that could be more effectively mitigated if the members regained confidence in the safety equipment they are issued and began*

## Step Three: The Grant Proposal

*initial knockdown efforts sooner. This rising cost for fire damage loss will eventually result in a new higher ISO rating and the accompanying increased home owner's hazard premiums they pay for insurance."*

*"Upgrading of our SCBA would also benefit neighboring communities, in that we are one of the few departments with a RIT unit (Rapid Intervention Team) in our area. With the upgrading of our SCBA we would be able to rescue trapped firefighters quicker and therefore cause a lower chance of loss of life. Currently we have to go over to the agency we are assisting and request an unused SCBA from them, which makes for an additional item that needs to be carried in. The upgraded SCBA would afford us the ability of "freeing up" a RIT member to assist in rescue instead of being a "pack mule." These SCBA would therefore increase our interagency interoperability within our service area."*

### Cost Benefit From AFGP Grant Proposal

*"The majority of our citizens clearly cannot provide any additional fees to keep their fire department within safety compliance factors. They are on fixed incomes and have very little net worth from which to draw. In our current state, we are on the borderline of losing our hard-earned ISO rating and this would cause an increase in their homeowner's premiums and deny affordable insurance to those who need it. Assuring that all of our firefighters are properly equipped, according to those standards, decreases the possibility of that occurring, extending cost benefit to them."*

*"Additionally, it is essential that we be able to supply our firefighters with dependable and reliable equipment for our suppression efforts to prevent excessive property losses and loss of life. When a citizen or firefighter losses their life there is an economic ripple effect throughout the community that continues to impact the area for many years to come and this results in economic hardship to the department through loss of taxpayer dollars and their income, which sustains the economic health of this community. Since many of these residents do not carry fire insurance, a loss of their home only contributes to their economic woes and creates a greater burden upon our community and State, in providing housing and sustenance monies from our overburdened State welfare programs."*

*"Our mutual aid partners will also realize the cost benefit in assuring that our firefighting equipment is not substandard and is totally ready to commit to any incident occurring in their areas as well. It does no good for volunteers to show up, if they cannot be safely committed to the fire because they are not safely and properly equipped. These dedicated volunteers become "just another rubbernecker" as they stand helplessly unable to assist."*

*"A full 20% of our budget goes towards workman's compensation insurance yearly. We must hold the line on our zero injury policy. We cannot afford any increases in our insurance premium cost due to a firefighter injury occurring needlessly. In properly equipping these firefighters with safe, proper PPE, we are mitigating*

## Grant Writer's Handbook

*some of that risk and at the same time assuring ourselves that we maintain a clean safety record so that our premiums do not rise."*

### Goals and Objectives

Remember

This section will help you organize your goals and objectives so that the reviewer knows exactly what you plan to accomplish. Goals convey to the reader what your overall mission is, while objectives provide more concise, specific ways your program activities should be measured. Objectives are also the minimum outcomes you plan to accomplish. It is important that you develop your goals and objectives before your program approach section is complete. This will keep the reviewer focused, reduce confusion, and enhance the flow of your document. Remember to let the reviewer know what you want to attain and how you will reach your criteria.

Goals and objectives are often easily confused with one another. One of the best ways to set this concept in your mind is to visualize a football field and the game itself.

GOAL: The goal of the game is to get the ball over the "GOAL" line into the end zone thereby scoring points.

OBJECTIVES: The hash marks, or yard lines, represent the progress you are making towards that goal. The short term goal is to gain 10 hash marks within four plays and you earn another 4 plays. If that cycle continues, eventually you cross the goal line and "achieve" the goal.

The yardage markers (objectives) give a "measurement standard" to the officials and spectators to see and determine what progress is being made towards scoring a goal and eventually winning the game. A grant reviewer needs to be able to see the same thing in your proposed project.

### Outlining Goals And Objectives

☐ Goals are the ultimate outcomes desired over a long period of time. Goals are general, broad and they convey the long-range benefits of your program. They are difficult to measure. Most grants contain 1-3 goals with 5-15 objectives per goal. Begin deciding on your goals by asking yourself the following questions.

1. How do I want to benefit from this program?

2. Long-term, what do I want to accomplish?

3. What outcome do I expect for the future?

4. What is my overall aim and ambition for this program?

## Step Three: The Grant Proposal

5. What does the RFP say about overall goals?

- Does it match with what my goals are? Generally, you should restate the RFP's goals in your grant.

6. How do my goals relate to my program approach section?

You should list your overall goals based on the above questions and what you are stating in your program approach.

☐ Objectives are the criteria that will measure your intervention and methods in order to reach your overall goals.

Unlike goals, objectives are measurable and specific. They help you determine if you are successfully meeting your goals. Usually there are multiple objectives for one goal. Always remember that for each objective you write, you must be able to evaluate the measure. So establish objectives that you are confident you can meet.

Consider these questions and comments:

1. What are my criteria for accomplishing each goal?

2. How will I determine or know if my goals are attained?

3. How will I measure success or failure?

4. Relate your objectives to your program approach section. It is important to remember that you do not mention any new ideas in your objectives that were not detailed in your program approach. Also, it is important that your objectives adequately cover what you have said in your program approach.

5. Use the outline you created in the program approach. Gather ideas about your objectives from your list. You should have at least one objective for each of your major program components or activities. Outline your objective topics—pick out 5-15 main program activities you plan to accomplish and write your objective for each program activity.

### Writing Goals And Objectives

After outlining your goals, you should write specific goals that convey exactly what you want to accomplish. Remember your goals will be general and broad. Goals never contain dates or numbers and should not be measurable. Consider using these verbs to help you emphasize your goals: utilize, assess, provide, build, serve, develop, translate, integrate, interpret, predict, prepare, make, contract, define, report, state, support, offer, attempt, join, visit, attend, share, increase, decrease, reduce, form, improve and coordinate.

www.HDGrants.com

Grant Writer's Handbook

Tips — After writing your goals, use your outline to write your objectives. You should have at least five concise, measurable objectives. Use some of the words above to assist you in writing your objectives. Contemplate these questions and comments below when writing your objectives.

1. Good, measurable objectives have most of the following components:

Checklist
- ☐ A number or percentage that you intend to increase or decrease something.
- ☐ A due date that you would accomplish this particular objective by.
- ☐ Consider using phrases such as "at least" or "a minimum of" for items you are measuring.
- ☐ Who the objective pertains to or the targeted population.
- ☐ Who will be responsible for these activities?
- ☐ Are you using objectives that are results-oriented and will achieve the desired outcomes?
- ☐ Relate the specific level of performance desired with clear descriptions.
- ☐ Make use of action verbs.

How do I write the objectives so they will ultimately accomplish my goals in a clear, concise way?

3. Consider the following objectives examples when writing your own.

- Poor: To provide in-depth training.
- Fair: To provide in-depth training by June 12, 2001.
- Good: To provide at least four training sessions by June 12, 2001.
- Excellent: To provide at least four training sessions for a minimum of 80% of the department in night vision surveillance, by June 12, 2010.

*Hints For Goal And Objective Writing*

☐ Avoid these common mistakes in a goal or objective setting:
- goals and objectives are not concise and clear.
- goals and objectives are wordy and too long.
- goals and objectives are set too low, sacrificing quality.
- goals and objectives are set too high and are unattainable or unrealistic.
- The objective are not consistent with the overall goals of the program.
- Time periods are too long or too short for objectives to be accomplished.
- Too much responsibility is given to one person to conduct the activities.

## Step Three: The Grant Proposal

- Barriers that would impede your completing the established goals and objectives have not been considered.
- Higher administration expectations are not being considered.
- The RFP is not being taken into account and as such the goals and objectives do not support the funding source's goals and objectives.

*Objectives cannot be measured and are just simply restatements of the goals.*

Remember

After writing your goals and objectives, use this checklist:

## Checklist for Goals And Objectives Section

- ☐ The goals are clearly stated and relevant to the problem, RFP, and program activities.
- ☐ There are at least five concise objectives that include numbers or percentages.
- ☐ Objectives include due dates or timeframes.
- ☐ The objectives are organized with numbers, so they are easy to follow.
- ☐ Dates are spelled out, while process number items you are measuring are not.
- ☐ Exact periods of time are used, versus vague dates.
- ☐ If percentages are used, the writer tells the reader what number the percentages represent.
- ☐ Avoids subjects that are simply focusing on purchasing in objectives
- ☐ Utilizes words that show a minimum criteria such as "at least" or "a minimum of."

Checklist

As a general rule you should try to set goals and objectives using a mindset of "under reporting and over achieving." Be realistic about what you can accomplish. You should always strive to "exceed" a stated goal or objective. This is a critical element that many in the Federal Grants system use as a "performance measure."

If you honestly feel that you can reduce a problem by 15%, then state you can reduce it by 12% and then if you do manage to achieve a 15% reduction you will be seen as an overachiever. This is a much better choice vs. stating that you would reach 15% and missing that goal by only 1%, which would mean that you will have failed to meet your stated goals and objectives.

*It is always better to be seen as an overachiever than to be viewed as underperforming.*

Must Do

In other words, in the future, they will look at your success or failure to achieve goals and objectives on previous grants as an indicator of how you would do on a future grant.

www.HDGrants.com

Grant Writer's Handbook

## Evaluation

This section helps you organize and write your program evaluation. Conducting an evaluation is important in measuring the quality and how well you performed with your grant. Evaluation is a way to determine the degree to which your program is meeting its goals and objectives.

**Remember:** Remember to show the reviewer how your evaluation will ensure that your outcomes are in line with theirs as are your goals and objectives. Having a solid evaluation system is important to prove that your program was, or is, successful and that the program should be continued or expanded upon.

**Tips:** Your program cannot exist without some evaluative method. How you intend to evaluate the program cannot be stated until the approach and objectives have been completed. Most reporting within grants will require some sort of measurements of what you are achieving as a result of the grant. This information comes from conducting an evaluation.

### Outlining The Evaluation

The purpose of an evaluation is to determine the effectiveness of your program. Your evaluation should be based on your goals and objectives, corresponding clearly with them. Use your goals and objectives to outline the main parts of your evaluation. Some of the things to think about here are:

1. How do I demonstrate that my goals and objectives were met? How do I evaluate each objective?

- List the possible ways to evaluate each of your objectives.
- Write and outline them.

2. What kind of change was desired? How do I know that this change was achieved?

3. How do I know that my program, or certain aspects of it, were a success?

4. Who can I find to assist me with the evaluation?

5. What type of evaluations do I need to use? There are three main types:

- **Process:** an assessment of administrative and program activities, such as number of services delivered. An example of this would be if you were seeking funds to deliver an educational type class to a group of citizens over a year's period of time. The "process" would be how many students did you state you were going to train and how many actually attended.

## Step Three: The Grant Proposal

- **Outcome:** an assessment of the final effects of program activities (measurement). In this type of evaluation you are going to measure if the training you delivered to each student raised their level of knowledge on the subject matter and would compare that to the baseline you established by testing those students prior to delivering the training.
- **Impact:** an assessment of changes in such things as behavior, knowledge, or skill development. This is the hardest of all the evaluations types to prove as "impact" is very difficult to measure. If you were delivering training to raise awareness of say Fire Prevention techniques, you would have to prove that the course curriculum actually caused the incidence rate of fires in your community to drop as a result of the training you delivered to the citizens.

6. What methods do I want to use to evaluate my program?

- It is important to remember to make sure your methods are not product oriented and are true evaluative standards. For instance, producing a videotape would certainly document the activities, but it does not truly evaluate the program form a standpoint of "did you actually reduce the occurrence of injuries occurring to your officers during the investigation of traffic accidents". Someone needs to evaluate the activities on the tape instead. In other words did the tape actually change the officer's tactics to be safer,
- Make sure the methods you choose can be conducted by a competent person. You certainly would not want someone who knows nothing about investigating traffic accidents to evaluate if your program to reduce officer injuries while investigating traffic accidents was effective or not if they did not truly understand what was being evaluated.

---

Be certain your evaluation techniques are not too sophisticated for the resources you have to evaluate. We have seen departments and agencies make statements such as" we will evaluate the effectiveness of this program by interviewing the citizens and measuring the impact the program has had on their attitude towards fire prevention in the home".

Tips

---

The statement literally says they would interview each citizen. If they only had 10 officers and a population of 22K people, how long do you think it would take for them to accomplish interviewing each and every citizen?

Some of the ways you should be considering for evaluating a grant program might include:

www.HDGrants.com                                                                                                                                          125

Grant Writer's Handbook

- ☐ Record keeping and documentation of data.
- ☐ Surveys and questionnaires: ask relevant people about the effectiveness of the program.
- ☐ Use of an independent evaluator or groups of other professionals.
- ☐ Comparison: compare your program outcomes to other similar programs.
- ☐ Pre- and post-testing.
- ☐ Reviewing or analyzing records and data in a systematic way.
- ☐ Conducting interviews.
- ☐ Experimental and control group comparisons.
- ☐ Observations.

### Writing The Evaluation Section

After you have outlined the topics for your evaluation, begin writing the evaluation section. Remember to make it clear and precise. Consider the comments below.

- ☐ Begin the evaluation section with a statement of who will conduct the evaluation.
- ☐ Using your outline, write one or more evaluation criteria for each of your program objectives. In most cases, it is better to have more than one method of evaluation for each objective.
- ☐ Make sure your evaluation process is clear and organized.
- ☐ One way to make your evaluation standard clear, is by listing each evaluation method or performance indicator under the corresponding objective.
- ☐ A second way, is to number your evaluation measures so that they correspond to the appropriate objective.
- ☐ It is important to include and involve people affected by the evaluation in the planning and implementation of the evaluation process.
  - ■ They are also stakeholders in the program
  - ■ Make them part of the "grant team"; gain their "buy-in" ahead of time.
- ☐ Re-read the evaluation section.
- ☐ Do you know exactly what will happen and what processes will take place?
- ☐ Also, can the outcome of the evaluation process be used to make the program approach or design better?
- ☐ Is there a logical order?

## Step Three: The Grant Proposal

### Evaluation Section Checklist

The following are suggestions to consider after writing your evaluation section:

☐ The evaluation section should begin with a statement of who will conduct the evaluation.

☐ The evaluation measures do correspond with the objectives.

☐ Each evaluation measure focuses on the qualitative or quantitative aspect of each objective.

☐ In most cases, each objective could have more than one method of evaluation.

☐ The evaluation includes a variety of ways in which to evaluate the project.

☐ The evaluation section does not repeat the objectives, but tells how the objectives will be evaluated.

☐ All evaluation measures are true evaluation activities and are not simply product oriented.

☐ Include how the evaluation's findings will be disseminated to other organizations and professionals, such as in-service training, presentation at conferences, publications, and brochures.

### *Performance Measures/Evaluation*

With the advent of the Internet and a computer now in two out of three homes in the U.S., the citizens in the US have become much more attuned to what and where the Federal government spends tax dollars on certain things. They are demanding accountability of how their tax dollars are being spent and they now have the means, through computer technology and the Internet, to check these things for themselves. The masses are literally becoming more educated. As such, Congress is demanding more information about the effectiveness of money being spent in grant programs and the actual impact that this spending creates or is supposed to create so that they can report to their constituencies. A method had to be devised that would allow for this information to be gathered collated and reported on before Congressional panels. Performance Measurement is the result of this and most Federal grants now require that certain Performance Measures be included into these programs and those results reported back to Congress when considering continuation of or to establish the need to have newer grant programs or to shut them down. Many Federal grant programs have now become "Performance Based Grants".

Efficiency and effectiveness are central goals for the administration of Federal grant programs in the United States. Efficiency means "is the funding well spent to accomplish

goals and improve whatever issue is being addressed". Effectiveness refers to carrying out the activities outlined in the program. The questions being asked were how to best achieve these goals. Apart from the obvious problem of determining the measurement criteria for a performance expectation there is a more difficult problem of determining what weight to give the finding and what changes need to be made to resolve the gap between expectation and performance.

Performance measurement must often be coupled with evaluation data to increase our understanding of why results occur and what value a program adds.

These are a central aspect both of the Government Results and Performance Act (GPRA) and of the Program Assessment Rating Tool (PART).

PART seeks to demonstrate that a program

1) has a track record of results and

2) warrants continued or additional resources

3) is demonstrating value to the taxpayer

**Remember:** Evaluations of various Federal grant programs vary from broadly descriptive to specific. Some grant writers perform process evaluations, others use outcome or impact evaluations, and still others perform both. Unless the agency commits adequate resources, evaluations will not achieve useful results. Assuming limited resources, it is unwise to commit to performing a large number of comprehensive process and outcome evaluations. There will not be enough resources, time, or an adequate product, and the result will be the perception that "evaluation just isn't worth it", when in fact the resources were spread so thin as to render the results useless.

Grant program evaluation may have many and varied purposes. An evaluation is used to test the viability of a unique and innovative program, it may be used to determine the advisability of continuing a program, or it could be used as a marketing tool to gain support for continuing a program.

Some programs seem to lend themselves naturally to what we think of as an "easy" evaluation - that is, some programs have easily quantifiable goals and, therefore, are easier to measure. As an example; it is relatively simple to measure the amount of narcotics diverted or a number of arrests. Alternatively, there are a number of other programs with "softer" goals which are more difficult to measure. Among these programs are treatment and rehabilitation programs, domestic and family violence programs, and prevention programs. The challenge to adequately evaluate these types of programs becomes greater now because of changing federal

## Step Three: The Grant Proposal

directions and priorities. It is important to examine these programs even when it appears that the data is "soft" and the technology eludes us.

The following guidance, using a criminal justice grant model, offers some assistance in this process of clarification, and is important in the development of measurable goals, objectives, and performance indicators. It is a process which may be applied to review a program's goals, or to programs applying for funding.

### A. Systems Improvement

Define the "system" to be improved - is it a segment (Judicial) or segments (Judicial and Treatment) of the system, or is it the entire criminal justice system?

Address professional networking - similar professionals improving the system by sharing tasks, etc.

- ☐ Address the larger system - Executive, Judicial, and Legislative branches
- ☐ Address policies and protocols of agencies - need for revision, etc.
- ☐ Education, in-service training for systems improvement
- ☐ How will improvement be evidenced?
- ☐ When will improvement be evidenced?
- ☐ Who will affect the improvements?

### B. Increased Coordination

- ☐ With whom will coordination increase?
  - Within an organization
  - With all components of the Criminal Justice System (CJS)
  - With components outside the CJS
  - With national efforts
  - With agencies being impacted
- ☐ Who will affect the increased coordination?
- ☐ What is it that will be increasingly coordinated?
  - Information
  - Money
  - Other resources - personnel, training, etc.
- ☐ When will the coordination occur?

☐ Why is increased coordination important?

☐ Is there an untoward effect anticipated?

☐ How, specifically, will coordination increase, and how will you know when it has happened?

### C. Crime Reduction

As with most missions/purposes, while the measurement of crime reduction may be quite easy, attributing that change to a source or cause is clearly more difficult. It is critically important that the following issues are considered:

☐ Current trends on incidence and prevalence

☐ Current awareness

☐ Awareness of public safety

☐ Satisfaction surveys - general population and victims

☐ Recidivism

A program planner's perception of what is desirable, or realistic, may not necessarily be that of those who administer and control that segment of the system. For example, establishing a substance abuse treatment program inside a prison may be a virtuous idea, but one which may not fit (or it might actually conflict with) the ultimate goals or policies of those who administer the prison. Alternatively, even if all policy makers agree that it is a great idea, the prison system might not be environmentally ready for such a move.

Virtuous ideas may not always be realistic ideas. It is always important to compare a program's goals with those of the segment of the career field in which the program will function. If this examination is actually accomplished, then the probability, or the potential for the program's success, is increased if the sponsoring governing body sees the program as being integral to its goals. This determination is accomplished through consensus program development and thorough examination of an organization's existing missions, policies, and goals.

## Establishing Performance Indicators

### A. Principles

A performance indicator is "an explicit measure of effects or results expected. It tells to what extent an activity has been successful in achieving, or contributing to an objective." When performance indicators are written, they represent the final and greatest level of specificity. If goals represent philosophy and objectives represent actions, then the

## Step Three: The Grant Proposal

performance indicators represent the anticipated results. The following principles apply to the development of performance indicators to be used in a grant application:

1. Indicators must follow from, and be directly related to, your program's objectives. Therefore, for each objective, a number of indicators must be written that describe what you anticipate or plan to be results of the actions described in the objective.

2. Indicators must be specific and clear enough to allow for measurement by someone that is not intimately involved in the development or management of the actual program. The indicators must also be reasonably attainable, given the design of the program and whatever constraints may exist.

3. Indicators may describe not only an exact result expected, but may also describe the degrees or gradations of achievement, and thus may be measured incrementally.

4. Indicators will describe each activity of the program, but some may be more important than others. Relative weights may be assigned to various indicators to adjust for this.

5. Objectives may be seen as the daily activities of those involved in the program, and indicators may be seen as what was accomplished at the end of the day, week, month, or year. The objectives will answer the question "How did you spend your time?" and the indicators will answer the questions "What was actually accomplished, how well was it done, and how often did it occur?"

### B. Maximizing Measurability

Being specific and clear are the keys to maximizing the measurability of performance indicators. If all the following standard questions are clearly answered in the performance indicators, then the program will have increased measurability which is ultimately the goal of having performance measures stated in the grant program application.  Remember

1. Who will be responsible for the performance? This question will focus exactly on which staff will perform exactly which functions. An organizational chart will help to illustrate who will supervise the staff or activity. This approach not only provides for greater performance, but also provides staff with greater job definition and accountability.

2. What exactly will be attempted? A good test for this question is whether or not the indicator is understandable by someone not familiar with the program. It should be clear enough for someone to perform the task with little or no further information.

# Grant Writer's Handbook

3. When, or over what period of time, will an action take place? A graphic illustration of a milestone chart will help staff to visualize when these various actions will occur, and it will serve as a useful tool in gauging and measuring program accountability. Also, it is important to note how much time is allocated to a particular activity. This allows for some measure of relative efficiency and could lead to cost-effectiveness measures.

4. How, or by what methods, will an activity occur? There are many methods which can be used to achieve the same results. Which methods will you employ?

5. Where will an activity occur?

6. Why will an action occur? Although this question will do little to increase measurability, its inclusion helps further define a program. If an indicator statement ends "in order to..." it offers staff a reason to do something and adds some degree of clarity.

## Timeline Management Plan

Remember

Most grant programs have a set time period during which to complete the grant program activities. This is called the "performance period". In many cases, this period will range from 1-5 years in length or can be as little as 6 months in some cases. The clock starts ticking on the day that your award is officially announced. In the world of performance grant reporting, you are required to complete the activities of your program within that time.

This may necessitate the inclusion of a timeline in your grant program narrative.

The timeline lets the reviewer know when your program activities will take place by using dates and time-periods. This timeline provides detailed information on program and administrative activities in a chronological order and provides the reviewer with another tool in which to evaluate the potential for your program to be successful and accomplished within the time periods allowed. It lends credibility to your efforts to have designed a comprehensive program and shows that you have considered some of the factors that could possibly affect your program's potential for success.

Once again, you should use your program approach section as a guide for what to include in this timeline. All of the activities mentioned in your program approach, should be reflected in this timeline. In addition, there should not be any new information or activities included in the timeline that have not been previously mentioned.

You can use this section as a primary planning and management tool, once your grant is funded. Whenever you add an activity; be cautious to add 1-2 months to your expectations to

## Step Three: The Grant Proposal

insure you can comply within the stated timeline. Remember that many unexpected problems (Murphy's Law) can interfere with or delay your expectations, so be realistic and anticipate that these problems can occur. After reading your timeline, the reviewer should have no doubts as to when and how long it will take to accomplish each section.

The following information provides more detail for constructing your timeline.

### Outlining The Timeline

| One of the first steps is to decide which activities you want to include in your timeline. Using your program approach, and the outline you created for it, list the major activities that will take place chronologically throughout your program. The following list will assist you in constructing that timeline. |
|---|

Tips

Have I included all of the activities that will occur in my program? Am I missing any? It is better to include a large number of activities, than underestimating. Generally, your timeline should cover approximately one page.

What additional elements should be included in the timeline that were not mentioned in the program approach?

You should include administrative tasks, such as ordering supplies and equipment.

Conducting evaluations.

Completion of the final reports.

Coordinating with financial persons.

| Always remember to include exactly what the RFP states should be included in the timeline. |
|---|

Must Do

4. Re-read your outline several times. Do the activities you are going to perform flow from start to finish?

☐ Begin considering your time periods that you will need in order to accomplish them.

### Writing The Timeline

After creating a basic outline, begin writing the timeline. Remember to be concise; this is not a place to be wordy. The timeline should not give too many details, but rather should cover all the primary points. The reviewer should already be familiar with your program activities from reading the program approach.

www.HDGrants.com

133

Grant Writer's Handbook

Descriptions of your program activities in your timeline should be limited to short, incomplete sentences.

- ☐ Sentences that are too long will confuse and frustrate the reader.
- ☐ Use your outline to organize your timeline.
- ☐ Use "action words" at the beginning of each activity.
  - Examples: organize, meet, review, sign, identify, update, develop, conduct, assess, begin, coordinate, visit, present, implement, reassess, conclude, order, submit, compile, convene, plan, execute, schedule, form, obtain, assign, target, solicit, report, establish, observe, analyze, maintain, create, generate, produce, promote and train, etc.

After writing your activities, consider what time periods you will use in your timeline.

- ☐ Program timelines usually begin about two months after the award date to allow for administrative tasks to be accomplished that are associated with receiving the award.
- ☐ You may want to include some of these preliminary activities, such as setting up checking accounts, ordering supplies and meeting with or forming advisory committees.
- ☐ What is the length of the award period?

Remember timelines should be realistic and be accomplished within the time period stated.

- ☐ Make sure your time estimations are spread out to completely cover the project period.
- ☐ What is a realistic amount of time to complete each activity? This question should be considered very carefully; allow for unexpected barriers that you may encounter such as weather related problems or backlogs or lead times of manufacturers if procuring equipment with the grant funds.

Most of the time, your activities are spread over the most common period of performance which is a 12-month period. On successive grants that you intend to apply for, only cover year one of your grant.

- ☐ Future year's activities would be covered in your continuation grant application that you would file in successive years.

Activities in the timeline are divided into different months, rather than specific dates.

---

No No  Avoid stating specific days of the months (i.e., October 10, 2001). This avoids painting yourself into a corner.
IE: If you stated that you would have the new truck in service by January 31st, and there was a delay at

## Step Three: The Grant Proposal

the factory that pushed your delivery date to February 25, then you are setting yourself up to fail on this particular objective by stating a certain date and then going past that date in actually accomplishing that activity.

Try using time periods instead such as : New truck will be in service within the first quarter of award. Using a time period from the date of award will prevent issues if the award date is pushed back.

- ☐ Several activities can take place in one month and simultaneously but you must be cautious here not to get the cart before the horse.
- ☐ How many months will be in your grant time period?
- ☐ Which program activities can reasonably be accomplished within one month or time period?

Divide your list of program activities into the appropriate months.

### Timeline Format

The format of your timeline is very important. Presenting your information clearly, is necessary to avoid confusion and misunderstanding of your timeline. You will accomplish this by carefully thinking the project through from start to finish.

---

Key Point #6 - Many grant RFPs will include a sample timeline of how they want the information presented; use their example if they supply one. You should be considering the following things while deciding the format that your timeline should appear in.

Remember

---

How can I organize my timeline so the appearance is neat and easy to follow?

Usually months are spelled out with the year beside the first stated month and are connected with each group of activities.

For clarity and ease of reading, it is important for your timeline columns to be straight.

4. It is important that your activities, within each month, be separated.

- ■ Is it clear how many activities there are?
- ■ Can I tell where the first activity ends and the next one begins?

The timeline chart below was developed as part of a grant application to establish a regional training facility, recruit and train staff, develop materials and hold a series of safety workshops.

www.HDGrants.com 135

### Grant Writer's Handbook

A commonly used tool is the timeline chart (GANTT chart). This chart is used to present a detailed list of all activities and their projected date of completion. Activities are usually listed in sequential order.

| Activities | Year 1 OR (Jan–Mar) | Year 2 OR (Apr–Jun) | Year 3 OR (July–Sept) | Year 4 OR (Oct–Dec) |
|---|---|---|---|---|
| **Staffing** <br> Recruit <br> Hire <br> Train | -----● | ---● | | |
| **Workshop Development** <br> Secure site <br> Develop agenda <br> Invite speakers <br> Prepare materials | ---------● <br> -----● | ---------● | | |
| **Printed Materials Development** <br> Hire graphics consultant <br> Develop logo <br> Design brochure <br> Print brochure | ---● <br> -----● | -----● | ----● | |
| **Evaluation** <br> Collect data <br> Analyze data <br> Write final report | -------● | ---------● | | ---------● |

You may be applying for only a one-year grant, in which case your timeline columns could be representative of quarterly progress versus years.

Free timeline templates are available from www.helpuplan.com/templates.asp

### Timeline Checklist

Below are some hints to help you review your timeline after it is completed.

- ☐ Timelines reflect detailed information on program activities presented in a chronological order.
- ☐ Timelines need to be realistic and achievable within the time period stated. By presenting this information it shows that you have "done your homework" and have thought the process through which is required in presenting a comprehensive proposal.
- ☐ The time estimations are spread out over the project period, and not bunched up in one month They need to reflect the entire grant period of performance.
- ☐ The months or time periods are spelled out and activities flow from start to finish

## Step Three: The Grant Proposal

- Timelines should begin about two months after the award date to allow for time to actually initiate the grant activities after handling some of the administrative tasks associated with being the recipient of an award.
- All timeline columns are straight allowing the reviewer's eye to track the activities smoothly.
- Timelines include all program approach activities and administrative tasks such as coordinating with financial persons within the organization, ordering supplies or equipment and completion of final report and evaluation.
- Each timeline is directly connected with each activity.

### Sustainability

Tips

When you are developing a grant program, you should think of it as though you were going to a bank to borrow money for a new business. A bank would require that you submit a "business plan" and any good business plan will contain information that would show the bank that you have done the research and have the experience needed so that they have a reasonable expectation of you making a profit and that you will have the ability to pay back the loan. A grant-funding source however, will not expect you to pay back the money so in all fairness it is reasonable to expect that you show them that you will be a good steward of their funding The funding sources have their own priorities and must show they are accomplishing them so they will always want to know that their money is achieving those purposes and that your program has a reasonable chance of success.

The primary reason that grant programs exist is to fund programs that address the social ills in our society and to act as a temporary bridge to fill the gap between the services needed and the money to successfully launch the program. A grant maker needs to know that even though the grant money will one day be gone, the program will carry on with a life of its own.

Generally, grants are thought of as "seed money". For those of you that may not understand that terminology, or its origins, let me explain.

When the frontiers of the American West were being settled, and the great "land grabs" occurred, the citizens who found their plot of land were absolutely destitute. They arrived literally with nothing but the clothes on their back in a covered wagon with the wife and kids, the family dog and the mule that pulled the wagon. They did not even have money to buy seeds to plant a crop.

The local bank would loan them the money to buy their seeds so they could plant a crop and grow it eventually taking it to market and selling it so that they could repay the loan. The understanding between the farmer and bank was that, when he harvested his first crop he would repay the loan from that the profits. The banker had to be certain that the farmer was smart enough to realize that he needed to save enough seeds from that first crop to be able

www.HDGrants.com

plant next year's crop and did not have to borrow money from the bank again - hence the phrase, "seed money"!

In this section, you will want to convince the funding source that your project is viable and not a waste of time and money. You should explain how you plan to sustain, or continue, the program once the initial grant funding is gone.

IE: Some hiring grants require you to retain an officer for several years, once the funding ends. Those of you in law enforcement might recall or remember that the UHP (Uniform Hiring Program) under the COPS program had this provision in their program guidelines. Fire service members can relate to this in the SAFER grant program. Some of the recent ARRA Stimulus grant and states for hiring had these type of requirements.

If your grant has a provision for this, you need to let the funding source know that you considered this and that you have taken positive steps to meet the requirement. In this case, you should:

- ☐ Include a resolution from your council or governing body that supports this action. It should include positive statements that would lead the reviewer to have no concerns that the governing or supporting body is adamant in honoring the terms of the grant award and will be diligent in attempting to meet those commitments.
- ☐ This section should give the funding source an idea of where the additional money will come from once the grant funding is expended. These statements should be realistic given the current economic conditions that might exist. Be cautious in this regards as to what you may be offering up as a method of sustainability. What worked several years ago under good economic conditions, may not work under the current conditions.

IE: 2-3 years ago you could use "historical future commercial or residential growth figures" as a justifying statement for sustainability. That argument today would be a moot point to most reviewers given the current "mortgage crisis" that exists and the resultant loss of tax base that is occurring. It will take years to return to levels which could realistically be considered to be relevant when using that argument.

Under the right circumstances some of the points you might wish to consider in developing a sustainability plan could be:

- ☐ Future tax base growth.
- ☐ Maturity of securities or investments.
- ☐ Retirement of debt service

## Step Three: The Grant Proposal

☐ Expiration of tax abatements from commercial interests

Tips

In the event you are obtaining equipment from the grant, you should include a statement explaining who will maintain the equipment in future years and how you intend to pay for it. Examples of ways to show sustainability for a vehicle for instance would include:
☐ Having the vehicle properly insured
☐ Having a routine vehicle maintenance program and a line item budget showing so
☐ Conducting or requiring Safe Driver Improvement courses
☐ Having facilities that will house the vehicle from the elements
The bottom line is you must show the funder that your program is a good investment.

Here is an example of a sustainability statement in a recent Fire Prevention and Safety grant from the USFA. This grant asked for a digital fire extinguisher training system, alarms and Home Safety blankets for a large University.

### Sustainability:

*The university has a solid reputation of maintaining our buildings, fire systems, and equipment. We have sufficient operational budget yearly to continue to fund our maintenance department and have adequate resources to purchase replacement parts and perform routine preventative maintenance so as to sustain the service life of the equipment requested. The university will save money on the maintenance of the fire extinguisher training system since we will not have to refill A, B, C dry chemical extinguishers. We project confidently that the smoke alarm system in the student apartments will last a minimum of 25 years. Our Housing and Residential Life facilities personnel will perform all routine maintenance and safety checks to ensure that the system lasts as long as possible. We estimate that the extinguisher trainer will last a minimum of 10 years. We have maintained our current system for more than 10 years and we are confident that we can continue to maintain this new system as effectively as we have in the past. Finally, we project that the Home Safety Blankets will last at least 10 years but, since there is no shelf-life restriction or mechanical or electrical components to wear out, or that will need replacing, this could be a serious under-estimate of their actual service life. We will sign-out the blankets given to off-campus students and they will be billed for their replacement if they fail to return their blanket at the end of the academic year. Likewise, blankets in the dorms will be monitored by the Resident Agents assigned on every floor.*

Sustainability is a critical element to any grant proposal regardless of the funding source. Private and Corporate foundations and State and Federal grant programs will need to see a plan based on sound principles and not conjecture.

Remember

www.HDGrants.com

Grant Writer's Handbook

## Exportable Products

In many grant programs, as a condition of funding, you will be required to produce "exportable products." We are not talking about a new "slicing and dicing" machine that you will export to be sold in China. Exportable products are sometimes also called "deliverables".

---

**! Must Do** — Key Point #7 - What this actually refers to is "knowledge gained". These may be research papers, reports, or documentary videos that describe the program's weaknesses and strengths and export the knowledge learned from the grant program to others locally, statewide, or nationally. Grants exist to solve problems. When you come up with an innovative idea to solve a problem, the funding source expects you to share that idea with others. A successful grant program should be able to be easily replicated by other departments, as this is how future grant programs come into existence.

---

Cooperative agreements and project grants are almost always going to require an exportable products section. Grants made through the NIJ (National Institute of Justice) are particularly prone to exportable requirements. The NIJ is the research and development arm of the Department of Justice. They exist to find new products or methods of dealing with problems involving criminal justice issues. Grants from this source were partially responsible for the development of bulletproof vests, bean bag guns and Compressed Air Foam systems for fire fighting. In essence someone somewhere thought they had a better idea or way of doing things in a more efficient or safer manner. The funding source gave them a grant so that they could develop, prove or disprove, that their idea would truly work and offer additional benefits.

Many private and corporate grant funders give money for research projects and expect results in return for their generosity.

The exportable product section, if required, is an important element in your grant. It details the specific products you plan to develop in your grant. Reviewers are generally impressed when the proposal shows how it will document successes and or failures, and how that information will be shared with others. Remember to convey that you will be giving something back in return for the consideration of funding your project.

### Outlining The Exportable Product

It is important to clearly state what products you intend to produce. Consider these questions and comments below.

## Step Three: The Grant Proposal

1. Look at earlier proposal sections, such as the program approach or goals and objectives. What items document information about your program and could be used as exportable products?

- Curriculum – maybe you are doing a training program and you have developed a training curriculum or .ppt presentation to teach this course
- Video tapes/CDs/DVDs- it is not unusual to make training tapes, CDs or DVDs in this day and age so that remote learning or individual employees can view it at different times in order to impart some skill or to teach a specific procedure or technique. It is also becoming commonplace to see training videos posted on You Tube for widespread distribution. Webinars are also becoming popular training methods for use with exceptionally large agencies with multiple stations to prevent officers or employees from needing to travel outside their zones of coverage which creates manpower problems. All of these techniques can be used to share information or knowledge with a wider target audience or to increase the efficiency of conducting training in this modern day and age.
- Program manuals – developing and printing of training manuals, on various techniques and procedures, is commonplace in grant programs that are geared towards training. These manuals represent "exportable products" that impart or further the value of the training to others beyond the initial target audience.

2. Consider other possibilities for exportable products that do not come from program activities (i.e., a news article). What could you generate to export knowledge?

3. The following are some common exportable products:

- How-to manuals
- Teaching curriculums
- Presentations and seminars
- Documentation of successes and failures
- News articles
- Professional publications , surveys, and reports
- Evaluation reports

Grant Writer's Handbook

### Writing the Exportable Product Section

It is important to write this section so that the reviewer understands exactly what exportable products you intend to generate. You should also show how you plan to transfer this knowledge.

Begin this section by restating the purpose of the proposal.

☐ This keeps the reviewer focused on your products.

☐ Use an example, such as the following:

The purpose of this proposal is to . . .

State why it is important to provide exportable products and how it is important to your program. Use these examples:

It is important that we disseminate the knowledge learned because . . .

This section shows how the program will export knowledge to others ...

Include a leading sentence that describes the exportable products you intend to produce.

The community will benefit from the following exportable products . . .

This program will produce (number) main exportable products . . .

The program intends to generate the following exportable products . . .

Next, describe each exportable product in detail.

☐ You may want to number and italicize the name of each product to keep this section organized.

Include these details:

☐ Description of the product.

☐ How the product will be disseminated.

☐ Who the exportable product will benefit.

☐ Who will be in charge of developing the product.

☐ When and how often the product will be shared.

After describing your exportable products in detail, show who will benefit and learn from your exportable products. Convince the reviewer that you will transfer the knowledge learned by conducting your program to others!

## Step Three: The Grant Proposal

### Exportable Product Checklist

Checklist

- ☐ List the exportable products you intend to produce (i.e., manual, curriculum, etc.).
- ☐ Show that the products can clearly export knowledge to other organizations and individuals.
- ☐ Exportable products document successes and failures so do not be afraid to list both.
- ☐ Section documents should clearly state to others how to replicate the project.
- ☐ Ensure that the section clearly shows how exportable products are helpful and how they will contribute to the body of knowledge regarding the areas they concern
- ☐ Be sure you use a method that is organized with numbers, etc. so the reviewer can follow your thought process clearly
- ☐ Assure the reviewer that you will be an effective disseminator of information.

### *Conclusion*

This section will help you organize the conclusion section of your grant. You should always keep in mind that the reviewer, at this point of the process, has been asked to read and digest a large amount of information. The conclusion provides the reader with a short restatement of the problem and how you plan to solve that problem. It gives a very general overview of everything you have previously presented in your proposal. The conclusion is one of the shortest sections of a proposal and includes just a few sentences to wrap-up your approach. Remember that this section is the last part of the narrative that the reviewer will read, so wrap it up on a positive note.

#### 1. Writing the Conclusion

The conclusion should be a brief summarization of your proposal, leaving the reader with a good feeling.

Remember it is important to use the actual name of your program or restate your department's name, so the reviewer can easily recall it when making the decision about who they are going to award.

Consider the following when writing this section.

1. Begin with an introductory sentence, using the name of your program.

- ■ [program name] represents another important step in . . . .
- ■ [program name] will reduce the effects . . .
- ■ [program name] will provide the needed . . .

www.HDGrants.com    143

- [program name] will enhance the lives of . . .

2. Restate the problem in one sentence. Review your problem statement for possible phrases and remind the reviewer why you are writing this proposal.

- The problem of _____ is continuing to grow . . .
- Without your help, the problem will continue to worsen . . .
- Our problem of _____ is increasing each day . . . etc.

3. Explain what your strategy is and what you plan to do about the problem. Tell the reviewer about your program one more time, reiterating how innovative your program is.

- This program will unite . . .
- This program will provide the basis . . .
- [program name] will increase _____ by enabling . . .
- [program name] will build the foundation for . . .
- This program will do the following things . . . etc.

Tips

4. Finally, include several positive statements at the end of this section. Build some excitement here, while clearly stating why your project should be funded. You want to leave the reviewer feeling he or she had to help! Make the reviewer say to themselves, "Yes, we need to give money — not to buy something, but to build a program." It should not be simply that you need to "buy an object", the "object" is needed to further a greater good or to achieve the desired results and actual solve the problem. Gently tug at the reviewer's heart strings.

- Together we can win . . .
- With your help we will . . .
- We can help people help themselves . . . etc.

Remember

5. Finally, remember to thank the reviewer, the company, and the program for their time and consideration of the proposal you have submitted to them. Reviewers are frequently unpaid for their time; they have their expenses covered but the actual time they spend doing this is substantial and mentally exhausting work. They agree to sit and read hundreds of application in order to determine who is best meeting the funding sources priorities and they usually volunteered to do this because they have a genuine desire to help. It is wise to point out to them that you recognize their efforts at bettering something within your community.

## Step Three: The Grant Proposal

### Conclusion Checklist

The conclusion should:

☐ Provide the reader with a very brief restatement of the problem and what you plan to do about it.

☐ Instill a good feeling in the reader who is about to score your grant.

☐ Voice a positive tone.

☐ Prove that the program does not end with the conclusion of program activity.

☐ Mention the program name again.

Below is an example of a conclusion paragraph in an Assistance to Firefighters Narrative Statement:

*The members of the Anywhere USA VFD and our community would like to take this opportunity to thank DHS USFA and FEMA for the opportunity to apply for this critically needed piece of firefighting apparatus. The award of this grant will no doubt be instrumental in assuring the safety and security of our poor residents, for many years to come. Our old fire truck has served this community for 35 years faithfully but, despite our care and attention to routine maintenance it has simply succumbed to old age and is now causing a financial drain on our taxpayers and our department. The continued use of this piece of apparatus is placing our firefighters and our citizens in peril. Without this greatly needed outside financial assistance, this purchase would indeed be impossible for us to attain. We believe we have presented a program that is a reasonable approach for obtaining a basic piece of firefighting apparatus. This is in keeping with the goals and stated priorities of the AFG program; we hope that you will agree with us and award us this request. Finally, we would like to thank you, the reviewer, for your dedication and time to serve the needs and safety concerns of the US Fire Service.*

### *Budget*

The basic components of a grant proposal budget are discussed here. To be clear here, this section deals with the budget of your proposed project, not the operational budget of your department.

---

The budget lets the reviewer know how you will be spending their money and how much your program costs. The budget must include a line item description for each component, supported by detailed information on how you calculated the cost of each line item. You should document the program's purpose for each expenditure and why the expenditure is important to your program. The project budget is often times requested by the RFP to be a separate page or pages of your narrative statement. This is done so that the narrative statement and the budget documents can be separated by the funding source, if need be, and scored or checked for accuracy by budget analysts or computer scanning.

Remember

---

www.HDGrants.com 145

Grant Writer's Handbook

The budget should be tied into your program narrative, and remember that a budget analyst, who may not have access to the program narrative, sometimes reviews the budget so it needs to be prepared with that in mind. It needs to be able to "stand on its own". Consequently, be very detailed and ensure that the budget can be reviewed alone. The reviewer or budget analyst should be able to read your budget and tell if your proposal should be funded or not.

A poorly constructed budget will undermine the funding chances of even the most exceptional program!

Budgets are cost projections. They are also a window into how projects will be implemented and managed. Well-planned budgets reflect carefully thought out, comprehensive projects. Do the homework and crunch the numbers. Follow the first rule of good management here and surround yourself with competent people. Many of us are simply not comfortable around mathematical formulas and are not "number crunchers or bean counters" but you can rest assured that someone connected with this grant program will be one of those people and they certainly will put your budget to the test.

You should enlist the aid of a budget person on your grants team, if you are not a budget person yourself. This is not the place to be making mistakes, as mistakes can be costly to you. Failure to consider all the costs can end up being the downfall of what might have been a very successful program.

Key Point #8 - Remember that you will have to live with this budget; there is no "do-over" button and you cannot go back to the funder and ask for more money simply because you forgot something. Think carefully about all the expenses you will have. If you will be hiring new people for example, do not forget that you may have to pay for classified ads to recruit them or medical physicals and screening tests. Also, take the time to get accurate estimates. If you will be printing a brochure as part of your program, do not guess at the cost. Call your printer and ask for a rough estimate. Audit costs, shipping and handling costs can all also be eligible expenses but, you must ask for them at time of application. Be thorough in your preparations

Most Federal grants require matching funds. This means your agency will contribute a percentage of the total funding needed to complete the project. In most cases, this will be actual dollars or what is referred to sometimes as " hard cash" but, in some cases, you can contribute "In-Kind" contributions. These are the soft dollar amounts that your agency or organization can contribute to the success of the project. If you are applying for Foundation funding, you should always include your In-Kind contributions as well as any actual dollars that are going into the project.

## Step Three: The Grant Proposal

In-kind contributions are gifts of goods or services instead of cash. They can include donated space, materials, or time. It can be the value of supplying a uniformed police officer and their squad car. The hourly wage you are paying that officer plus the benefits and costs associated with having a fully equipped squad car are all "costs" that are incurred as a result of supplying them. Even a volunteer firefighter who donates time on Saturday to go around and install smoke detectors, has an in-kind value associated with that (according to the Presidents Points of Light Program that time is $18.50 per hour in value). If you list In-Kind contributions as income in your budget, you must also show the corresponding expenses. If someone gives you something at a major discount, you would show the whole expense and then list the portion being donated under In-Kind contributions.

IE: a major retail chain agrees to allow you to purchase smoke detectors with your grant award and will extend a 50% discount to you in support of the community and your department's efforts to stop residential fires. The smoke detector has an actual retail value on the shelf of $30 and since you are doing a grant program the store agrees to sell them to you at a 50% discount or only $15 each. You would explain in the budget that the cost to purchase the item is $15 but you would also show an in-kind value of the discount as a part of the overall project cost totals; $15 dollars coming from the grant funds you are asking for and an in-kind donation from the store of $15 for each smoke detector.

**In-Kind contributions can be important for three reasons:**

It shows all the ways in which the community is supporting your project, even though not everyone is giving cash.

It shows the true cost of the project — what you would have to spend without the community support.

If you want to show In-Kind for these reasons you can either show it in the budget, as above, or simply add a footnote to the bottom of the budget, like this:

"This project will also receive more than $3,000 of In-Kind support from the school district, participating businesses, and various professionals."

If you are applying for a matching grant, the In-Kind income may sometimes be used as part of the match if the RFP specifies that it can be used. If you want to use In-Kind contributions as part of your match, then you must put a dollar value on them and put them in the budget. Funders who provide matching grants may have policies on how much In-Kind expenses you can use in your match and how it must be documented.

Grant Writer's Handbook

### Cost Benefit/Budget Justification

The budget justification should be the monetary rationale for the proposal, and it should explain why you need funding for the items requested. You should include the benefit to the community as well as mutual aid partners and any other group that will benefit from your receiving the requested funding. Include an explanation as to how each group will be changed and prosper from the funded items, or project.

The following provides a checklist for your program budget.

Checklist

1. All figures add up, and it includes a formula to let the reader know how the final numbers were calculated.
   - ☐ Mileage to and from airport @ .26 per mile x 20 miles x 2 trips = $10.40. Never allow the reviewer to try and figure out how you arrived at a certain figure. Just as surely as the night is dark, if you allow them to use their own calculation formulas they will arrive at a different sum and that is not good for your application.
   - ☐ Keep in mind that one small error or change in a figure on your budget page could affect other numbers or items in your budget. That would present a conflict or discrepancy; something that you wish to avoid at all costs.
   - ☐ Your budget should always add up and balance. Remember you are asking the finding source to give you money and if you cannot make the budget figures add up on paper during the request, what assurance does the funding source have that you would be able to properly account for all the money once it is given to you. You are demonstrating your ability to be a good steward of their money and a stickler for details here.

2. The budget should not include big, round whole numbers (i.e., $10,000).
   - ☐ Are costs reasonable for the market, or too high or too low?
   - ☐ Show item prices in your budget.
   - ☐ Avoid large, whole numbers, because it implies you are guessing at the cost.
   - ☐ State that you will follow departments or local and state procurement and bid policies.

3. Explain why the budget item is needed and the activity relating to the purchase.
   - ☐ Tie this into the program narrative.

4. The budget has at least three columns: requested funds, matching funds and total funds.
   - ☐ You can also have local donations, other grant funding, or In-Kind match.
   - ☐ In-Kind match is the value of your contribution to the program. This could be office space, personnel, supplies, training, or anything your agency is supplying for the program.
   - ☐ In your budget narrative, make sure you are clear on where the matching funding, In-Kind donations or any other funds are coming from.

5. Explain where local donations were obtained.

6. The budget lists subtotals for each main section (i.e., Subtotal Fringe).

www.HDGrants.com

## Step Three: The Grant Proposal

- If you have more than one item listed in a section, you should subtotal that section to make your budget as easy to read and understand as possible.
- Make it clear exactly what you are asking for and the purpose.

7. Some of the main sections headers of the budget include: personnel, fringe benefits, travel, equipment, supplies, contractual and other. Generally, it is not a good idea to use "other or miscellaneous" columns in your budget. If you don't know exactly what you are spending the money for, why should a funding source be expected to provide that money? Use of misc or other columns, without proper explanation, can leave a reviewer thinking that if money is going to be misappropriated to benefit a particular individual then this would occur right here. If you choose to use these column headings, be sure to explain in detail what is included in those amounts. Remember funders do not provide "extra" or "reserve" funding for your project, they are only interested in funding documented and necessary expenses.

8. Always use whole dollars without cents. There can be several reasons to do this:

- Grant funding awards usually are never awarded in an exact amount such as $125,475. 87 . It would be awarded simply as $125,476.00. It is acceptable to round up to nearest dollar.
- eGrant applications sometimes have "character counts" associated with entry of your grant and the submission. If you put .00 or .10 after each cost being listed you are using up an extra three characters each time you do this and you very well may need those characters elsewhere in your application to explain something in more detail.
- Finally, think about this. If you use exact dollar and cents figures, and you have 30-40 entries with those figures stated, the chance for a mathematical error in your calculations becomes much more likely to happen. Simply rounding up leaves less chance for a mathematical error to occur in your calculations.

9. All columns and headings are lined up and centered. Make it easy for a reviewer to track things with their eyes.

10. Use a table or spreadsheet to format your budget. If you are using MS-Word, be sure to use tab stops instead of space bars when formatting the budget. In some of the new E-grant systems, you must check how your budget will be imported into the online application. There have been cases where formatting was in issue–tabs or tables could not be used. In this case, you have to use a dash or = sign. Such as:

(6) Complete Sets SCBAs @ $3,890 each = $23,340

(25) Complete Sets of Turnout Gear @ $1,635 each = $40,875

Notice the use of ( ) for the number of items, this keeps the number you are asking for clear. The $ sign is used and commas, too, so numbers are clear to anyone viewing them.

11. The budget includes all items mentioned in the program approach. Re-read your program approach and be certain that you have justified each and every item in your budget. Also, check to make sure all items and costs that the program will allow are included.

Example: You are requesting a GPS computer crime mapping program

- You have the cost of the software and the necessary computers in the budget however, you forgot to include training on the use of this new software. No funding source will allow you to come back for more money once the application has been filed. Nor will they award you additional funding, once you have been awarded the grant. In this example, you may end up with a wonderful tool for your department, which no one can use.

## Grant Writer's Handbook

Many grant programs application packages may provide an actual example of how the budget information should appear.

> **! Must Do**
>
> Key Point #9 - If an example is used, be sure to use the example that they provide.

Your budget might look better, read easier, and be more attractively formatted but remember what we said above about the budget document being separated from some grant narratives. They might be reviewed by a budget analyst separate from the rest of your grant. If you change the form that they are asking you to supply data on, you may very well make it impossible for them to use Optical Character Recognition (OCR) or scanning programs designed to do computer evaluation and budget calculations. If they give you an example, always use their example.

The chart below is an example of what a typical budget worksheet may look like. Look at the chart and see if you can tell what was left out of this budget.

| Sample Budget | Requested Funds | Local Contributions | In-Kind Contributions | Total Costs |
|---|---|---|---|---|
| A. Neighborhood Watch Coordinator (part-time) development of informational packets, seminar curricula, teaching and coordinating seminars @ 15 hours per week x 50 weeks @ $13 per hour | $ 9,750 | | | $ 9,750 |
| **Subtotal Personnel** | 9,750 | 0 | 0 | 9,750 |
| **II. Equipment** | | | | |
| A. Computer equipment including CPU/monitor, laser printer, and software for word processing, brochures, and curriculum. This will be provided by the city. | | | 2,905 | 2,905 |
| B. Camcorder/VCR/Monitor will be used to develop and record seminars. | 1,155 | | | 1,155 |
| **Subtotal Equipment** | 1,155 | 0 | 2,905 | 4,060 |
| **III. Travel** | | | | |
| A. State Travel includes transportation for Coordinator to training sites: 708 miles per month @ .25 per mile = $177 X 12 months | 2,124 | | | 2,124 |
| **Subtotal Travel** | 2,124 | 0 | | 2,124 |

## Step Three: The Grant Proposal

| Sample Budget | Requested Funds | Local Contributions | In-Kind Contributions | Total Costs |
|---|---|---|---|---|
| **IV. Contractual** | | | | |
| A. Office space for project coordinator already exists through the city for preparing curricula and seminar information. $300 per month X 12 months | | | 3,600 | 3,600 |
| B. Telephone for line to communicate with participants and organize locations: $41 per month X 12 months | 492 | | | 492 |
| C. Seminar space donated by local FOP: $98 per month X 12 months | | 1,176 | | 1,176 |
| D. Printing 5,000 brochures = $325 total; 100 educational packets w/50 pages @ 3.5¢ per page = 77¢ per participant X 15 participants = $11.55 x 12 classes = $138.60 | 639 | | | 639 |
| E. Mailing Lists purchase lists to send to target groups: 5,000 labels @ $100 per 1,000 = $500 | 500 | | | 500 |
| F. Mailing of brochures and educational packets – 5,000 brochures @ 32¢ each = $1,600; 100 educational packets @ $1.28 per packet = $128 | 1,728 | | | 1,728 |
| G. Professional Video will be developed by Radford University | | 4,372 | | 4,372 |
| Subtotal Contractual | 3,359 | 5,548 | 3,600 | 12,507 |
| **V. Supplies** | | | | |
| A. General Office supplies such as pens, disks, paper, etc. $82 per month X 12 months | 720 | | 264 | 984 |
| B. Video tapes to record training seminars: 2 seminars per month X 12 months = 24 seminars X $1.78 per tape | 43 | | | 43 |
| Subtotal Supplies | 763 | 0 | 264 | 1,027 |
| TOTAL DIRECT COSTS | $ 17,151 | $ 5,548 | $ 6,769 | $ 29,468 |

What key element is missing from this budget? The fringe benefits for the coordinator. If the agency applying receives funding, they will have to pay the fringe benefits themselves because they were not included here. If they cannot, then the money will have to be returned or the grant will have to be refused. How would your planning or budget committee react to a mistake like this? This is not an area of your grant application to be

! Must Do

www.HDGrants.com

### Grant Writer's Handbook

making mistakes in. Use proper due diligence here to assure that this section has been checked, rechecked and checked again before submission.

### Checklist for Budget Section of grant application:

- ☐ 1. It should be able to stand alone during the review process.
- ☐ 2. Utilize whole dollars only. Do not use dollars and cents.
- ☐ 3. The budget should support your program.
- ☐ 4. There should be a detailed narrative describing each expenditure.
- ☐ 5. Do the math; be certain that your calculations are correct and that everything adds up and agrees with what you may have stated in the program narrative. Do not have discrepancies between the two documents.
- ☐ 6. If you are supplying a budget be sure it is formatted attractively and accurately.
- ☐ 7. Estimate real costs; resist the urge to "pad" or "hedge" against information or rising materials costs.
- ☐ 8. It should be driven by the program.
- ☐ 9. A good budget will have fewer changes or amendments after the grant is funded.
- ☐ 10. Present the actual formulas outlining how the expenditures were calculated.
- ☐ 11. Present a reasonable and credible picture.
- ☐ 12. List and discuss any major purchases in both the budget and in the program approach.
- ☐ 13. Follow the funding organization's format always if provided
- ☐ 14. Avoid using a "miscellaneous" or "other" column.
- ☐ 15. Provide multiple year line item budget (if needed).
- ☐ 16. Include increases each year, i.e., salary.
- ☐ 17. Your budget should be carefully planned and realistic.
- ☐ 18. Provide strong documentation for the need for money.
- ☐ 19. Explicitly detail each budget calculation.

# 6. Step Four: Alternative Funding

## Corporate/Private Foundation Solicitations

### Concept Papers for Foundations

Almost all corporations and large business concerns in the world have charitable programs or foundations. They have these for public relations reasons and for tax advantages. Likewise, many wealthy individuals in the U.S. are afforded the same advantage, and they set up private foundations such as the Bill and Melinda Gates Foundation

Remember

Your agency's eligibility to apply to these funding sources is usually the first problem that you will have to determine. Most Foundations cannot give their money away to anything but a not-for-profit or non-profit entity or they lose their tax advantage which is the primary driving force behind establishing or having a charitable foundation in the first place.. For those reasons, looking at the "eligibility" requirements is one of the very first things you should do when seeking these types of funding streams.

Prior to the events of 9/11 public safety concerns, for the most part, were not eligible for these. They received Federal money or tax based revenues and were viewed with an inaccurate perception from the public, as though they had everything they needed to do their jobs.

Since 9/11, the public has become much more acutely aware that public safety agencies are for the most part, underfunded, under equipped and overworked. It is common knowledge that terrorist and criminal elements outspend public safety agencies at the rate of as much as 10:1. These elements are typically using state of the art equipment which is technologically advanced and public safety agencies are always in a constant state of "catch up" due to lack of tax based revenues. Thankfully it is now becoming more common for many of these companies and individuals to fund public safety programs.

The public has also had an epiphany in finally realizing the connection between adequate public safety available and the relationship that is directly related to the ability of a community to grow economically. In years past, the most common question asked by a new family unit before buying or moving into a new town was " How are the schools?" Currently that question has been relegated to a lower position of importance to a potential home buyer and

Grant Writer's Handbook

has been replaced with " How long does it take to get a cop, fireman, or EMT to my door when I call 911?"

Even retailers have now discovered the nexus of protecting their potential customers by supporting the efforts of public safety agencies. One of the largest retailers in the world has actually studied how much money the average family spends in their stores over a lifetime; $800,000.00. It is not difficult to see that a family of 3 that perishes in a fire because the local fire department did not have the proper equipment represents a tremendous dip in their overall log term profits.

When you are trying to determine eligibility, it is important to know what status the IRS considers you. If your organization has a true non-profit status designation ( 501c3) , as many Volunteer Fire Departments or Rescue and EMS organizations are set up, you will not encounter too many eligibility problems. However, many of you will find that as a local unit of government you may only be considered a 501c type organization, but lack specific C3 status. The key here is to read the eligibility section very closely for what it says exactly. It is not unusual to encounter language such as this:

- ☐ We fund 501 organizations, public schools and units of local government
- ☐ We are limited to assisting non-profit 501c3 organizations only
- ☐ We fund not-for-profit or non-profit organizations only

As you can see, there might be a big difference from one program to another and each of those statements may or may not apply to you. One of the better ways to think of this is to determine if you are specifically excluded vs. being eligible. In other words, is their language such that it specifically says "not us"?

The important thing to remember is that if you see that you are in a gray area and not positive of your eligibility; ask them! The authors have presented grant applications to companies that previously had never thought about funding a public safety agency before, and have not only gained permission to apply but have done so with success.

Sometime it is necessary for you to point out why a charitable funding organization would be interested in hearing about your project by explaining it to them in terms that may not have previously considered. That is why, as previously mentioned, it is important to form the nexus between your need and the funding sources need.

IE: Several years ago while returning from a training workshop in the NW I was seated on the flight next to a VP of a large company that grows trees for producing wood and paper products. As our conversation developed into what we each did business wise I asked the

## Step Four: Alternative Funding

person if their charitable giving foundation funded Volunteer Fire Departments. He replied "no", that they were not within their funding priorities. After several seconds of contemplative thought, he turned back to me and asked "Why? Should we be?". I pointed out to him that the trees they grew were in essence a crop tied directly to the profits of the company. I also stated that I believed it took 12-15 years to grow a tree to the size that they used in their production of products and he agreed that both of those statements were true.

Now, for those not in the know, pulp trees of pine are typically grown in "blocks" of trees with thousands of trees crammed into acre-sized blocks and these types of companies have hundreds of thousands of acres growing all over the US.

I asked the executive if he had ever seen a forest fire start in one of these blocks of trees and he replied that he had only seen the aftermath. He agreed with me that these types of fires are devastating to them and that it takes 10-15 years to recover the losses incurred as a result of them. I then asked him who he thought responded to the forest fire when it starts out as a small lightning strike and the smoke first becomes visible to a citizen driving by on the road who calls 911 to report it. He reckoned that the call went to the State or US Division of Forestry. I corrected him in saying that although the State Division of Forestry or US Forestry might eventually be called and get involved, in reality the people who got notified were usually the local Fire Department. Since most of those tracts of land they plant trees on are located in rural areas it was more than likely that a Volunteer Fire Dept would respond to the call first.

I pointed out to him that most of these smaller VFDs would not have a modern 4x4 vehicle that was properly equipped to drive off-road and reach the seat of the fire to extinguish it prior to it becoming a full conflagration and burning up thousands of his trees and that his company's profits were literally "going up in smoke."

I told him about how a fire fueled by twelve inches of pine needle fuel on the forest floor would quickly race into the tree tops and then create a firestorm as it surged at 60 miles per hour in a crowning fire. He was told that in one hour this type of a fire could conceivable consume or destroy 10-15 acres of trees valued at $20 per tree and how that translated to a $400,000 loss to his company.

I then explained that the local VFD would be standing by helplessly, unable to effectively fight the fire, because they could not afford to risk taking their normal $225,000 fire engine off road and close enough to be effective for fear of it getting stuck in the mud and then being burned up by the fire. I also pointed out that it is difficult to maneuver a 30 foot long fire engine in pine trees planted at 2,000 per acre. He was told that even though they needed a 4x4 properly equipped brush truck to fight that fire, they survived financially year to year

www.HDGrants.com

Grant Writer's Handbook

on the donations of their local citizens and that it would take these volunteers more than 125 boot drives to raise that kind of money to buy a $125,000 brush truck.

I painted a vivid, imaginable picture for this executive so that he could see the relationship that the VFD meant to his company and their profits. As he reached in his pocket for a business card, he replied to me " If you have a VFD in my area where we grow the trees and they are in that kind of need, have them contact me."

I have since done so and his company now donates regularly or allows VFDs to access their grant funding. All it took was forming that nexus between the local VFD and his company for him to realize that maybe their funding eligibility was too limited and they would be better served by allowing these types of agencies to also apply.

Lesson learned? Sometimes you need to explain why you fit their priorities in order to be eligible or to get them to make an exception for you.

Must Do — One of the things you must always remember when dealing with and funding source and particularly Corporate / Foundation grants is to "Know Your Target Audience" that will be reading your grant.

Remember — Key Point #10- Remember that those that review private foundation and corporate grants are unlikely to be involved in your profession. They will not understand your jargon or technical terms associated with your career, so avoid using them. They will more than likely be upper class, highly educated and you must factor that in when writing your grant.

These private and corporate charitable foundations can be found through a search of the Internet. Look for companies in your area that do business there or have employees living in your communities. They usually try to target their charitable giving into these areas. Find the company websites and look for their charitable activities. You may find keys to this hidden in sections of their websites entitled "Community Support", "Giving Back", "How We Help", or "Community Involvement".

Tips — When applying to Foundations, keep in mind that they are big picture thinkers, interested in programs that will benefit the whole community in most cases. The type of funding we usually see from Foundations promotes the arts, literacy programs, community services, and conservation projects. So, projects like search and rescue, problems with at-risk youth and programs that involve multiple partners stand the best chance of winning funding.

If you decide to apply to foundations, there are different rules that apply, as well. Foundations often ask for a concept paper or a letter of inquiry, which usually consists of a

## Step Four: Alternative Funding

cover letter and a two- or three-page summarization of the proposal. A one-page budget may serve as your third page.

Typically when seeking funding from these sources you will utilize what is known as a shotgun approach. That is to identify 5-10 companies with funding priorities likely to be receptive to your program and then send a concept paper and letter of inquiry to all of them to see which one bites at the apple, so to speak.

The most widely accepted format for these papers calls for 1" margins, justified paragraphs, Times New Roman or Arial 12 pt. font, using bold for headings only. And, bullets are preferred to listing items in sentences with commas.

### Letter of Inquiry or Executive summary

Your letter of inquiry should be in standard, business-style format on your agency letterhead. Use quality stationary type paper with some linen content and of decent weight ( 22+ lb) and a brightness factor of 93 or higher. Have this letter signed by the head of your agency.

We recommend including one paragraph addressing each of the following components:

- ☐ **Introduce your agency.** Tell the funding source who you are and where you are located as well as what you do and who you serve. This description may be based on your organization's Mission Statement.

- ☐ **Introduce the project.** The next paragraph is a brief big-picture summary of the project you are proposing. Address needs, the program goal and offer an overview of program activities. Pique the interest of the reader here; compel them to read the attached Concept Paper.

- ☐ **Establish agency credibility.** Convince the funder that you are a worthy cause. This may be accomplished by briefly offering evidence of project stability and sustainability, or briefly describing ongoing programs or past grant projects that you have successfully executed.

- ☐ **State the bottom line.** Let the funder know how much the project will cost.
  - You may present the total project cost, followed by the amount you are requesting from this funder (if seeking funds for only one component).
  - You may state the project total and then list the amounts required for various project components, allowing the funder to choose a level of support.

Grant Writer's Handbook

- ☐ You may ask for support for the entire program (always mentioning in-kind agency and community support).
- ☐ **Close with a "thank you."** Thank the funding source for their consideration of your program and let them know you will be contacting them to discuss the possibility for funding.

## The Concept Paper

Your Concept Paper is 1-2 pages in length and may include a third page delineating the budget. None of these pages should be on agency letterhead but you should use quality paper. It can be helpful to call attention to the sections of the Concept Paper with the use of section headers after you have compelled the reader to keep reading with an inspirational opening statement. Readers who are scanning a stack of proposals will appreciate your clarity, and headers improve your chances of capturing their attention.

One paragraph should address each of the following components.

- ☐ **Problem Statement:** Your opening paragraph must succinctly explain the community need, while also compelling the reader to continue reading your proposal. Begin with a "punch," if possible. This punch could be a dramatic statistic or a "plucking of heart strings" quote. Support your problem assessment with statistics from independent sources, and include a paragraph presenting the statistics with the most relevance and impact. Be sure you have clearly explained the problem to the reader, as well.
- ☐ **Goals And Objectives:** A brief, clear presentation of your project goal with an overview, or synopsis of the related objectives, will establish the basis for your project activities.
- ☐ **Project Activities:** In this section, you want to mention the major service-delivery components of the program. There is little emphasis on administrative tasks, with the exception of the planning and oversight committees or use of a task force, which speaks to community involvement and support. There should also be a section to briefly mention sustainability and evaluation, if relevant.
- ☐ **Management Plan:** It is helpful to include a paragraph addressing oversight of the project as well as a few key elements from the timeline, particularly regarding when you will begin providing services. Also consider outlining your evaluation plans, i.e., who will be responsible, how information will be used and how results will be monitored.
- ☐ **Budget:** Typically, your budget is presented on a separate page. You may prefer to limit the financial discussion to the cover letter (the "bottom line" paragraph). This will depend on the size of both your program and your request. Most of the time, an

## Step Four: Alternative Funding

attached one-page budget will serve you well. A budget will further clarify program components and reflect positively on your planning and management skills.

Keep in mind that, typically, it's the affluent "upper crust" members of society who contribute to these foundations. They did not get rich and powerful by making poor decisions or by failing to plan thoroughly. They will expect the same from you, and your only chance to demonstrate your competence is in the way you present your proposed project.

Now that your Concept Paper is assembled into one document, you must analyze the document length. Compare the total length and the length of each component to any maximums specified by the funder. Remember that content is much more important than the word count! Funders will forgive an extra word or two if you have told your story convincingly.

On the following pages are some examples of successfully funded concept papers.

---

**Fire Prevention Concept Paper**

United Way of Tompkins County's Youth and Philanthropy

"Protecting At-Risk Seniors Through Fire Safety Education"

Founded in 1823, the Ithaca Fire Department provides emergency service protection to the City and most of the Town of Ithaca (excluding Northeast Ithaca and the Village of Cayuga Heights), serving approximately 60,000 people, and an area of more than 30 square miles. A division of Ithaca city government, the department serves the town through a fire protection agreement. The department responds to approximately 3,500 emergency incidents each year, providing not only fire suppression service but also emergency medical service and a variety of technical rescue services. Its mission: To save lives and protect property.

As well as responding to emergencies, the department works hard to prevent emergencies before they happen, through the code enforcement and public education programs of its Fire Prevention Bureau, as well as its specialized Juvenile Firesetter Intervention Program, which works with children at risk because of fire setting behavior.

The Fire Prevention Bureau seeking your assistance has, within the past year, added three personnel whose responsibilities are solely dedicated to fire prevention. The bureau has instituted an active public assembly inspection program and is working to diversify its public education program to specifically target at-risk groups and to refine its focus, taking its educational program out to those populations, instead of leaving it to their own initiatives to come to the fire station. The incidence of fire occurrence in the department's service area has decreased significantly in recent years; a trend that we are confident reflects the success of our fire prevention activities.

Totally supported by city funds, which are declining, the Ithaca Fire Department finds that budgetary constraints severely limit its ability to develop needed new fire prevention education initiatives and to purchase the instructional materials needed to deliver the programs. Its primary goals include

www.HDGrants.com

## Grant Writer's Handbook

implementing an ever-expanding fire prevention program to meet the needs of the community, especially those most at risk - the very old, the very young, and the very poor.

The Ithaca Fire Department seeks your support to enable it to initiate an intensive fire prevention education program focused on the elderly within its service area, the City and Town of Ithaca. Both national data and our local experience confirm that senior citizens are among those with the greatest risk of fire, including fatal fires. The elderly are more likely to be smokers, more likely to be infirm or with reduced physical and/or mental capabilities, and because of this they cannot respond as quickly and effectively in case of fire.

For example, one woman suffered serious burns and smoke inhalation from a fire at Titus Towers last November, injuries which could have been prevented had she and her neighbors at the housing project been better educated regarding what to do in case of fire. Our experience has been that this population, however, is definitely responsive to educational efforts helping them to be more fire-safe, and we are confident that an effective education program carries strong prospects for success.

Program summary:

Through this year-long program, the Ithaca Fire Department will deliver a focused fire safety education program to well over one thousand senior citizens in the community, in cooperation with the living units and agencies serving this population. These programs would be delivered at sites including the following:

Titus Towers I and II

Ithaca Housing Authority

West Village, Maple Avenue, Center, and Plain Street low-income living units

Linderman Creek complex

Ellis Hollow Road elderly housing complex

Tompkins County Senior Citizens Alliance Council.

In each educational program, participants would:

- See a fire prevention and safety video, specifically targeted at the senior population
- Learn fire prevention suggestions and tips from fire safety educators who are trained fire fighters
- Participate in a round-robin discussion involving their peers and the educators
- Receive written handouts, which specifically target the senior population, to reinforce the fire safety message
- Receive a smoke detector for his or her home, without charge, as needed. Through assessing questions and comments made during the round-robin discussions, educators would be aware of participants' level of understanding of fire safety concepts and which concepts needed reinforcement for that group.

Community-wide, the project's impact will be assessed through reviewing local statistics and trends involving this population after the program's completion, specifically whether the incidence of fire-related fatalities and injuries experienced by the population have declined, as we are confident they will.

Program elements and requested budget:

## Step Four: Alternative Funding

The Ithaca Fire Department requests support for program materials and a nominal amount for administrative support. The department will support personnel cost of the fire safety educators, as an in-kind contribution.

Video: "Senior Fire Safety with Jonathon Winters" $ 359.00

Handouts: "How to Prevent Fires" (for ages 65 and older) 360.00

Quantity: 2,000

Smoke detectors: Quantity: 60 (@ $6/each) 360.00

Administrative support: 121.00

TOTAL AMOUNT REQUESTED: $ 1,200.00

We believe the Youth and Philanthropy Council should fund this program not only to enhance the fire and life safety of those at risk in this community, but also to show its support for cross generational contact and unity between youth in this community and one of the community's greatest resources, its older people. Our elder population serves as a resource that this community should value, preserve, and cultivate, and we at the Ithaca Fire Department are confident that this project, should it win your support, would constitute a key element in initiating that process.

Supporting documents:

A. Program budget (see above)

B. Agency budgets for 2000 and 2001 (attached)

C. Board of Directors

As a municipal agency, the Ithaca Fire Department does not have a Board of Directors, per se, although its board of Fire Commissioners has authority over facilities and volunteer issues in the department. The department's Assistant Chiefs will soon assume responsibilities as an oversight board for development issues. These officers are listed below:

Assistant Chief Raymond Wheaton, Jr., Fire Marshal

Assistant Chief Glenn Wanck

Assistant Chief Guy Van Benschoten

Assistant Chief Leon LaBuff

Assistant Chief Michael Schnurle

# Grant Writer's Handbook

DOMESTIC VIOLENCE CAMERAS

January 15, 2005

The Donation Corporation

100 Parkway

Spring, TN 37174

Dear Sir or Madam:

The City of Long Beach is the fifth largest city in California with a diverse population of 481,000 with 4.3 million visitors each year. The city covers 50 square miles, has several major freeways, an airport, tourist ship terminal, State University and one of the busiest ports in the world. Long Beach Police Department's vision is to become California's safest large city secured with a mission to be a crime fighting, financially effective organization trusted by the community and its employees. The Police Department is staffed with 958 sworn and 485 non-sworn positions that mutually protect and serve the citizens of Long Beach.

The Police Department is committed to reducing violence and keeping the community safe. Acquiring domestic violence cameras will ensure that domestic violence injuries are documented while the Officer is at the crime scene. Injury photographs are beneficial to the Detective investigating the case, the Attorney filing the case, and to the Judge and Jury that are determining the outcome of the allegations. Convictions are key to reducing the repetitive nature of the crime. Attached is a concept paper detailing our program request for your review.

The department is well respected by the community and other police agencies across the nation. In addition the agency is technologically advanced, well trained and provides full service capability. Employees are active in the community and committed to the organizations that help the department provide a full array of services to the community.

The funding requested to purchase 180 camera kits is $20,000. In addition, even partial funding would be greatly appreciated. All program funding will be employed exclusively to purchase camera kits. Your consideration of this request is greatly appreciated. If I can be of assistance, please contact me or my Chief of Staff, Commander J. J. Craig at (562) 570-7301.

Sincerely,

Anthony W. Batts

Chief of Police

AWB:SF: sf

C:\msword\letter\050103-03b

Attachment

Domestic Violence Camera Program Proposal

Long Beach Police Department

100 Long Beach Police Department

Long Beach, Ca., 90802

Contact Person:

## Step Four: Alternative Funding

Stephen Fritch, Criminalist

562 570-7319

Stephen_Fritch@ci.long-beach.ca.us

### Problem Statement

Domestic violence is a complex problem involving relationships, economic conditions, emotions and entangled social issues. The police department is tasked on a daily basis responding to domestic violence calls for service, investigating the cases for court filing and assisting with the court prosecution.

Since domestic violence case filings are in most instances based on observable injuries, it is imperative that the injuries get properly documented. Photographs tell the story and unlike testimony, they cannot be forgotten, altered, or changed over time. Domestic violence cases without photographs are difficult to file and/or to obtain court convictions. Since convictions stop the cycle of violence, photographs are essential to prevent future crimes and injuries. This program will purchase and issue cameras to Patrol Officers so that they can document domestic violence injuries while at the crime scene.

### Goals

Goal 1) Obtain domestic violence cameras, cases and gray cards

Goal 2) Distribute domestic violence cameras, cases, gray cards and photographic supplies to patrol officers for use on domestic violence calls.

### Project Activities

Currently, the police department has approximately 100 officers that have been issued domestic violence cameras.

These cameras are beyond their useful life (7 years old) and in immediate need of replacement. New cameras will be distributed first to officers with issued cameras that need replacement and the remainder will be issued to patrol officers that would like to become involved in the domestic violence photography program. At the time the cameras are issued, training will be provided to explain the cameras use and features.

### Management Plan

Within 90 days of funding, the cameras, cases, and gray cards will be ordered. Once received, approximately 45 cameras will be distributed to patrol officers each three months until a total of 180 cameras have been issued.

### PROGRAM BUDGET (Estimated cost for equipment and supplies)

The requested domestic violence program budget is $20,000 which will be allocated to purchase 180 point and shoot cameras, cases, and gray cards. The anticipated program costs are as follows:

35 mm point and shoot camera with case (180 cameras @ $100/each) $19,400

Gray cards (200 cards @ $3.00/each) $600

Total    $20,000*

* Price includes shipping and taxes

Individual Camera Kit Price ($111.10)

Grant Writer's Handbook

35 mm point and shoot camera with case $99.64

Gray Card     $3.00

Total     $111.10 each

SMF: smf

When approaching corporate or private foundations for funding support, the use of a Concept Paper and Letter of Inquiry will usually result in one of the below listed results:

A polite "thanks but no thanks" letter indicating that they are either out of money or that your project fails to fit their current funding priorities.

An email response may arrive containing a user ID and password directing you to a company website where you would be allowed to access their application for assistance or formal grant application to either download or, in some cases, complete it online.

An application packet and formal invitation to submit to their program may be sent to you.

Many times a check simply arrives in the mail

In the case of this last scenario happening; we have seen on many occasion, depending upon how many initial inquires were sent out, that it is possible to have several checks arrive for the same project. This raises the moral and ethical question of "do we need to return that which has already been funded?" Yes, you do have an obligation to discuss that with the funding source but, before doing so, you should consider the following.

**Must Do:** If you are utilizing a good grant strategy you should always have a list of projects on hand that are also on your agenda to pursue. These projects are typically the kind that represent a line of thought of " it would be nice to have this item or complete this project but, it is not of critical need to us".

Private foundations, corporate entities and even Federal Grant programs do not particularly like to take money back, once it is given and this is for several reasons;

- ☐ The money is usually given with an underlying reason for the entity to claim a tax credit. If they take that money back, they lose the ability to claim the credit.
- ☐ Administratively and logistically a check, once written, creates a problem for the funding source in re-assimilating the money back into the grant funds.

## Step Four: Alternative Funding

☐ Money left over at the end of a funding program, that has not been committed to the purposes originally intended, tends to indicate a "lack of need", and can result in less funding being initially appropriated for those purposes.

What you should be prepared to do in these cases is to contact the funding source and indicate to them that prior to receiving their contribution, another entity stepped forward and fulfilled that need for you. You should then state to them that before you return their donation, you wanted to tell them about another worthy project that you are also seeking to fund and that you wished to ask them if you can use the original donation towards that project.

We have discovered, through experience, that most funding sources would rather let you use the money towards another eligible project, than to go through the administrative logistics of having the donation returned to them.

Tips

Additionally, having a list of smaller potential projects that you are trying to work on provides an additional benefit for you in regards to citizens wanting to make a donation to the department in appreciation for some deed that has been performed for them or for a loved one.

Most people, by simple human nature, like to take single credit for accomplishing things. You should use that trait to your advantage. When a citizen walks in or calls and asks to make a donation, I have discovered that having a "project list" typed out stating the associated costs to fund all or part of a project, ( generally under $5K) is a great idea to have posted on a white board in your office or a clipboard hanging on the wall.

I hand the clipboard to the citizen or ask them to look at the white board and then tell them we want to make sure that their donation goes where they think it would do the most good and ask them to designate where their money should be put to use.

Amazingly what sometimes happens is this. When the citizen sees the whole project cost laid out for each individual component and also as a whole, he or she frequently decides that the entire project is worthy of funding and within their means and they agree to fund that whole small project themselves.

IE: An EMS agency was utilizing this approach and had a clipboard at the ready with several smaller projects listed on it. A citizen came into the executive director's office wishing to make a $2,000 donation to the department for rendering aid to one of his relatives during a medical crisis. The ED handed the man the clipboard and asked him to designate which project he would like his money to go to. The man pondered the list for a few minutes and

www.HDGrants.com

165

## Grant Writer's Handbook

saw a project where the agency was trying to raise funding to purchase and equip 4 bicycles for their paramedics to use during large festivals and events where their rescue units could not navigate due to pedestrians. Cost of each bike was right at $1,000. When the man saw this he asked for his check back and tore it up. He then proceeded to write a check for $4,000 in order to fund the entire project and get it instituted immediately. Problem solved!

Another example of this tactic was realized by a Search and Rescue agency seeking to equip their swift water rescue team. Their team had been called into service during a severe flood that found one of their more affluent resident's home completely surrounded by rising floodwaters and the very foundation of his home eroding from under him. He and his family were literally trapped until rescued by the efforts of the team utilizing a borrowed boat and antiquated equipment.

The team, during debriefing of the incident realized they were woefully underequipped to deal with the issues they had faced and noticed areas that were in dire need of attention in regards to team equipment and personal safety devices for their members. They designed a project and placed it on their board as a future program to deal with if the $27K in funding needed to purchase the equipment became available.

Several weeks after the flooding incident, when the floodwaters had receded, the homeowner who they had rescued, walked into their station house wanting to give a donation for rescuing him and his family. He noticed the project on the white board and wrote a check to fund the entire project right there on the spot.

This is not unusual and occurs more times than ever reported in the newspapers, because many benefactors wish to remain anonymous and without publicity surrounding their generosity.

### Alternative Funding Strategies

#### "If They Don't Know It's Broke, They Can't Fix It!"

For many years, and particularly true with public safety agencies, the administrators of these agencies have taken an attitude of internalizing all problems out of the view of the public eye. We did not want to be seen as "whiners" especially where public tax money was concerned. This attitude forced many agencies to never speak out when money issues started becoming apparent in the department. It wasn't until an actual crisis existed that the issue was reluctantly brought to the city commission and/or aired in a public budget hearing.

## Step Four: Alternative Funding

This tactic usually resulted in at least several comments from citizens asking why we had waited to tell them something was wrong and wondering why we had not brought it up before. The unfortunate answer to most of those inquiries was that it was not brought up in its initial stages because the Chief or administrator was worried that they would be viewed as a poor money manager and face consequences as a result.

We have also similar type problems arise when going before boards or commissions to ask for permission to file for grant assistance only to be told that there was no money in the budget and the agency was denied permission to even file for a grant funding opportunity.

There is a simple truth associated with the fact that if someone does not know something is broken, they will never offer to fix it.

Remember

Benevolence is defined as "a disposition to do good or a generous gift or kindness". Benevolence surrounds all of us in every community in the U.S. You need only watch the outpouring of support evoked from even the poorest of the poor after a natural disaster or catastrophe occurs anywhere in the world to confirm this fact. U.S. citizens donate more financial aid to those in need than any other country in the world. Look around you and watch as even the youngest of children will donate pennies – for example to the victims of the recent earthquake disaster in Haiti or the Katrina disaster in New Orleans.

Why do people donate to those causes? Publicity! They were deluged with information 24/7 for days on end to garner support. We, as public safety agencies administrators, should not ignore that lesson. People and citizens will "step up to the plate" but only if they know there is a problem. We simply must not be afraid to let our citizens know that indeed something is broken and needs to be fixed.

It does not take a full-fledged "investigative reporter" to bring something to the forefront of the public's focus. In this day and age of instant electronic communication, all it takes is a blog or a notice on a website. A video posted on "YouTube" documenting a problem or the condition of things can do wonders for letting the public know your needs and concerns. This is new age thinking and it works. Do not be afraid to use it to seek out a benevolent benefactor who might just come to your aid.

Getting the equipment you need is sometimes as simple as making a few phone calls or sending a letter.

Tips

Here's how one small department got what it needed. This is a story from a Constable in the State of Texas.

www.HDGrants.com 167

Grant Writer's Handbook

The Golden Hour Was Wasting Away

Constable Ed Miller covers a 2,000 square-mile territory in rural Texas. He provides legal process serving, search and rescue efforts, and criminal law enforcement to the residents of his area. On December 28, 2004, he was on patrol and was dispatched to an oilfield explosion and fire, which had occurred in a remote area 13 miles south of Albany.

The location was far off the beaten path and in the "back forty" so to speak. Upon his arrival, Ed discovered two men, badly burned as the result of the explosion. He and rescue personnel determined that a Medivac helicopter was essential for the survival of one of the men.

A Medivac was called. While en route, it began experiencing difficulties in finding the exact location of the officer and the patients. Although in radio communication with the helicopter, the pilot was still confused, as were the personnel on the ground, as to where each of them were located. As a result, precious minutes of the "golden hour" were wasting away for the survival of the burn victim. The constable and a local fireman scrambled to the top of a close-by hill, located the helicopter, and visually vectored it to their location. The end result was that the injured men were safely transported to hospital and recovered. That situation turned out well, but Constable Miller knew that something had to be done for future situations.

Locator, Locator, Locator

Constable Miller contacted us after this incident. What if he were in a similar situation again, where ground and air personnel had trouble identifying location? What if he ever needed to call in a backup officer to assist him?

The solution was simple: Constable Miller needed a hand-held GPS locator unit. If he had been equipped with such a unit, he could have relayed location information to the helicopter pilot with a quick GPS reading. The pilot would have plugged this data into his navigational equipment and would have landed right on top of them within minutes.

A simple, $150 piece of equipment could give Constable Miller the edge, the extra few minutes, he may need to save someone's life.

However, Ed's budget would not allow the purchase of such a device. He turned to us for help.

Did You Talk To Wal-Mart?

Did you know that Wal-Mart, and many other corporate entities, have a very strong commitment to public safety agencies that serve their customers and protect their stores and employees? Approaching area businesses is something we often suggest to departments.

In this situation, Wal-Mart was the natural choice because they sell GPS devices. Constable Miller was instructed to do the following:

- ☐ Write a letter to his local Wal-Mart, explaining what had occurred
- ☐ Take the letter to his local store and seek out the manager
- ☐ Introduce himself to the manager and explain his situation.

The letter and his conversation would inform the manager that Constable Miller was seeking assistance from Wal-Mart

## Step Four: Alternative Funding

### One Letter = Problem Solved

Here is the letter that the Constable presented to Wal-Mart:

HANDHELD GPS

OFFICE OF CONSTABLE
EDWARD A. MILLER

CONSTABLE

SHACKELFORD COUNTY TEXAS

PO BOX 877

ALBANY TEXAS 76430

(325) 762-2232 EXT 112

FAX (325) 762-3966

January 6, 2005

RE: Request for Assistance w/ Public Safety Need

Dear:

Please allow me to introduce myself; my name is Edward Miller and I am the Constable of Shackelford County, Albany Texas. My area of coverage encompasses 2,000 square miles.

I am a public servant tasked with the responsibilities of Civil Process Service, the enforcement of State of

Texas criminal, traffic law, and first response to emergencies. I deal with highway accidents, hunting accidents and injuries, lost children and adults, industrial, ranching and oil field emergencies.

As I am sure you are aware, most counties in North Central and North West Texas are comprised of rough and rugged terrain that requires air-medic ambulances to respond to evacuate the injured and the use of 4 x 4 vehicles to access them.

These incidents sometimes occur far off the roads and in areas where distinguishing direction or trying to navigate to them is extremely difficult. I was recently involved in just such an incident but, this is not the first, nor will it be the last time that I will be called upon to perform these emergency life saving duties.

On December 28, 2004 I was dispatched to an oil field explosion and fire with two burn victims 13 miles south of Albany on the South Green Ranch. A life flight helicopter had to be dispatched to air lift one victim to a burn unit. None of the responding rescue team had a handheld G.P.S unit with which to give the helicopter a coordinate so that they could arrive where we were. A fireman and I had to scale the closest hill and spot the helicopter and then direct the pilot to our location by radio.

This resulted in critical "golden hour" minutes being wasted. Fortunately, the man was eventually rescued and is reported to be in fair condition and is expected to recover from his injuries in a burn unit in Dallas. It is only a matter of time until this deficiency in our operating capability is less fortunate and results in a life being lost.

www.HDGrants.com

## Grant Writer's Handbook

We are constantly involved in situations like this all in my county and the equipment to do the job in a more proficient manner would be a life saving asset. My office has a very limited budget and we are unable to purchase this relatively inexpensive but nonetheless very critical piece of equipment. I am asking for Wal-Mart's assistance in obtaining a hand held GPS device so that when needed, we can quickly determine our exact position and relay this time saving information to other responding units and air evacuation personnel.

The citizens of Shackelford County and I thank you for your consideration

Sincerely,

Edward A. Miller

Constable Shackelford County Texas

Shortly after this introductory meeting with the Wal-Mart manager and delivery of this letter, Constable Miller received a call asking him to return to the store. When he got there, Constable Miller was handed a brand-new handheld GPS unit for future use.

Problem solved, and all it took was one simple letter, plus a few minutes to explain the situation.

### Talk With Your Community

How could this work for your department? As public safety agencies, we should not be afraid to make our problems public. Too often, we expect the citizens to know what it is that we face on an everyday basis, but they don't — unless we inform them.

- ☐ Donations, such as Wal-Mart's donation of the GPS device, can mean fewer department requests for tax increases.
- ☐ Donations can often be written off as tax deductions.
- ☐ Discussions of the challenges your department faces make the citizenry more aware, involved and interested in your department and, therefore, more likely to help.
- ☐ Anonymous donors abound everywhere. We need only look at the number of hospital wings, children's advocacy centers, and libraries that are built through the efforts of anonymous donors.
- ☐ We hear the plight of many departments seeking to renovate or build a new stationhouse, yet there are very few grants that will undertake this. Consider publicizing your plight and asking for assistance from the public or from corporate America.
- ☐ Offer to name your new fire hall after a local citizen in exchange for a donation of the land to build on. Many childless widows and widowers, for example, seek to leave a legacy behind.

## Step Four: Alternative Funding

☐ Talk with the citizens, businesses and organizations in your community, and let them know what the problems are.

This is a strong argument for having a proper media relationship and for publicizing the plight your department is facing. Wal-Mart, K-Mart, Target and many others have policies in place that encourage local managers to help their local communities in meaningful ways.

Sometimes, all it takes is letting them know that you have a problem. It may seem that ours is a thankless job most of the time, but when the chips are down, someone usually steps up to the plate to help.

Here is another example of how this strategy can work for you.

### From Discussion To Harley Davidson

One day in a coastal jurisdiction with a lot of beach tourism and traffic, a patrolman was sitting in a small department office writing a report when a citizen walked in off the street and asked to see the department's motorcycle unit.

The officer replied that they were so small they could not afford such a unit. The officer and the citizen then discussed how weekend beachgoers caused total gridlock on Saturdays and Sundays, making patrol in a squad car almost impossible. The patrolman suggested that the matter was out of his hands and should be addressed to the city council.

The next week, that same citizen walked into the station and handed that officer the keys to a brand new, fully outfitted, Harley-Davidson Police motorcycle. As it turns out, that the citizen was a retired Ohio State Highway Patrolman who had worked for their motor unit for more than 30 years. He could not stand the fact that the town where he retired didn't have a motorcycle to work with. His only stipulation to the department for his gift to them? He wanted it ridden by his home at least once per week! A small price to pay for a very generous donation.

Like Constable Miller and Wal-Mart, this incident offers a valuable lesson. Keep the public informed, because if they don't know it's broke, they can't help you fix it!

On the following pages are a few sample letters that have resulted in donations:

**PERSONAL WATERCRAFT LAW/LOAN PROGRAM**

August 13, 2004

John Smith

Watersports, Inc.

www.HDGrants.com

171

# Grant Writer's Handbook

Anytown, USA

RE: Personal Watercraft Law/Loan Program

Dear Mr. Smith,

I would like to personally thank you for taking time from your busy schedule to speak with me regarding the innovative Personal Watercraft Law/Loan Program. As you are aware, the Police Department is tasked with patrolling and enforcing laws along the miles of riverfront area within our jurisdiction. This includes the recently enacted "No Wake" zone.

At the present time my department is unable to actively patrol these areas or offer meaningful timely assistance, in the event of an emergency situation arising in these areas. The recent and future growth of the City is rapidly increasing along these riverfronts, with a large marina in the development stages at this time.

It is the department's desire to be effective in delivery of our public safety services and at the present time neither the department nor City is financially able to afford the purchase of a boat or similar type water rescue craft to accomplish this mission.

On behalf of my department, and the citizens of our City, I would like to request that our agency be considered for participation in this program with the loaning of a personal watercraft for official usage of this department.

My department will comply with all requirements stated by the agreement and will maintain full insurance coverage on the watercraft as required. All personnel who are assigned to patrol with this watercraft will be properly trained and certified in its use.

Participation in this program will allow our department to offer a higher degree of safety to our residents and the tourists who frequent our area. The quick launch and ease of towing will be of great cost benefit to the City in that we will not require a special vehicle to tow the watercraft. This will also allow us to respond to a water emergency in a much timelier manner. As you know, seconds and minutes can be the difference between life and death in a water-related incident. The addition of this type service should encourage further growth and other business interests to locate to our area.

Please consider this to be our formal request for participation in this needed public safety program. Any assistance you may be able to offer this department would be gratefully appreciated.

Respectfully,

Chief of Police

---

4 X 4 SUV-TYPE VEHICLE

RE: Request for Assistance

Dear Sir,

I have recently been appointed as the full-time coordinator for the County Emergency Management. During the past ten years this position was a part-time position and our County officials have recognized the need for a full-time coordinator to increase the preparedness and response ability to disasters that would affect our families and loved ones.

## Step Four: Alternative Funding

As the newly appointed director, it is my responsibility to prepare our citizens and government officials to properly mitigate any disaster, manmade or natural, in an efficient and orderly manner. This requires a tremendous amount of time, effort, and resources to coordinate all of the agencies and citizens to work as a cohesive and effective team. It also requires financial resources.

Our County has been able to fund a full-time coordinator with a living wage, and I have dedicated myself to the task at hand. Unfortunately, funding the salary and benefits for this position has resulted in a funding deficit in regards to equipment purchases for the immediate or near future.

As you can imagine this position and the tasks I have been asked to accomplish requires a tremendous amount of time (which I have) and travel to coordinate the many agencies and citizens needed to accomplish this mission. I am currently driving a 1992 Jeep Cherokee with more than 150,000 miles upon it. It is in poor condition and needs almost weekly maintenance to keep on the road. It is also too small to carry the equipment I must maintain and have available to set up a mobile command center at a disaster scene. I need to obtain a large capacity 4 X 4 SUV type vehicle, in order to accomplish my mission.

I am seeking the donation of a suitable vehicle which would assist in accomplishing this task. If your dealership would be capable of offering us any assistance in this endeavor, I and the citizens of this County would be most appreciative. We would, of course, prominently mark this vehicle as being a donation from your dealership in support of the community and your customers. We would also seek positive "media" coverage of your participation and generous donation. I believe this would be a great opportunity for you to express your community stewardship as well as being a tax deductible and advertising expense for your business.

I would welcome the opportunity to discuss this with you in detail at your convenience and your due consideration to this worthwhile project would be greatly appreciated. If you have interests in this project please contact me at the above number. Thank you for your time and consideration.

Respectfully,

Coordinator; County Emergency Management

## *Think Training Aid, Not Equipment*

Training takes up a large quantity of our time and our budgets in public safety work. We must constantly meet certification standards that are mandated to us. Mandatory training standards are also often mandated without consideration of the funding mechanism to pay for this training. That is why often times grant programs are offered that encourage training and because of this, we can locate another source to obtain that vitally needed, critical piece of equipment. Let us show you how to use this tactic to your advantage to gain that equipment.

IE: You are part of a Fire and Rescue Department that has a need to obtain rappelling equipment for high angle rescue work. This is not a high priority item on traditional grant programs so you are currently without a way to fund the equipment to complement and be able to perform this part of your technical rescue work.

## Grant Writer's Handbook

There is however a priority within the Assistance to Firefighters Grant program to complete training to the compliance levels of NFPA 1001 for FF1 and FF2 standards and ropes and knots are a part of that particular training curriculum. It is feasible to write a grant application that would offer to teach the ropes and knots course utilizing your certified instructors. This program would be offered 4 times per year and any fire department in the surrounding 100 sg. mile area would be free to send their FFs to this course where they would be taught the ropes and knots section of the training .

Now, if you are going to teach a course about ropes and knots, what would you logically be expected to have to accomplish that? The ropes and the associated equipment to accomplished this with, right? You could request at least some of the equipment needed for your rappelling needs by categorizing them as a "training aid" needed to teach the ropes and knots course. In other words, you made this equipment necessary , in order to carry out the scope of the project you were trying to do.

Now, what do you think happens to those ropes and equipment when they are not being used during the 32 hour of classes that you will run during the year? A little clue! They will not be sitting in a box in the bottom of a closet. They will be on the trucks and available for use.

You have to be reasonable here though. They are not going to fund a new Fire Engine for you, just to teach a course on pumping a fire engine. Always remember, your request must be reasonable!

### Solve Someone Else's Problem With Your Skills

Tips | Being the grant writer for the police department or the fire department in a municipality does not mean that you are limited in the skills needed to assist another department within your city or area in applying for a grant. A grant, is a grant, is a grant!

Grants will solve some problems but they will not solve all financial problems within your own department. If you find yourself stuck in this area and cannot locate a grant to resolve the issue within your own career discipline, get outside your area and look elsewhere. Perhaps you can look at the overall city budget and see that the Parks & Recreation Department is scheduled to build a new park next year at a cost of $125,000.

If you do some research and look around, perhaps you could locate a funding source to obtain those funds and then offer to assist the Parks & Recreation Dept with applying for the money to build that park. If you were successful, that could mean that the money that

## Step Four: Alternative Funding

was going to be appropriated for that park project could be transferred to your budget to buy those new squad cars you need.

IE: Here is an example of using that scenario above, with a little bit of a twist, but which was nonetheless effective and showed ingenuity and creative "outside the box" thinking on the part of the grant writer in resolving a problem facing his police department.

The grant writer was in a small town police department and like many departments these days, was losing their trained personnel to surrounding agencies for as little as a $1,000 per year increase in salary. This was in turn costing the department $15-20K in new training and recruitment costs every time this was occurring. The grant writer was unable to find a grant which would pay salaries.

Faced with no other choice, the grant writer chose to bring this request before the City Commission during budgetary consideration meetings in a request for $12K in money to allow a $1,000e per year increase in salary for all the department's officers. In a public hearing on the proposed yearly budget and in front of a packed auditorium filled with citizens the grant writer made the pleas and posed the argument for the increases in salary and the request, as expected, was promptly denied. The grant writer was astute enough not to leave the podium at that point and asked the Commission to state a reason, publically, for denying the request. They immediately replied that the public works department had to replace the city's only backhoe that year and that this was going to take a $150,000 and there would be no room for salary increases. The grant writer left the podium.

The next day the grant writer went to www.govliquidation.com, a website where surplus military and government equipment is auctioned off much the same as on eBay, and began searching. Lo and behold a nice large backhoe was found on the site being auctioned off less than 100 miles from their location. The backhoe was everything that the public works director stated he was looking for in this piece of equipment and actually had more features than he originally envisioned. According to the hour meter the backhoe had very low actual use hours on it and had come from a USAF military installation in Germany that had been shut down.

The next day the officer took the public works director to the site where the backhoe was located and showed it to the PW director and asked him to check it out. The PW director stated that this was a really good backhoe and had very little use on it so far. The grant writer asked him if it would serve his purposes as a replacement and the PW director said it would do nicely for that task. They went inside and were told that the current bid was $13,500. The grant writer determined that the PW director still had $15K available in his budget for equipment and they put in a bid of $15K. They won the bid and the PW director called for a

www.HDGrants.com    175

Grant Writer's Handbook

semi-truck to haul the backhoe back to the city. Problem solved within existing budget for PW, immediately!

Now for the rest of the story…

Where do you think the grant writer was during the next budget hearing? Why he was back before the commission again and in front of the same citizen audience he had been in front of the month before. He now showed the photos and the receipts for winning the auction to the commission and the audience stating that in essence he had just saved the city from spending $150K and had saved the city $135K . The commission was, of course, exuberant about that saving…..then he asked what their excuse was now for not giving his officers a raise? The audience behind joined in and began chanting "why not".

Guess who got their raises that year!

## 20: Proposal Format

**No No** — This section provides you with a checklist for your proposal format. Considering the appropriate format for your proposal is very important. A messy proposal will turn off reviewers, no matter how good the content is.

**Remember** — Key Point #11 - The proposal's appearance reflects directly on how well organized and professional your agency is. So, put some time into the format and make your proposal look good! You should always follow the format specifications, if indicated in the RFP.

Below are typical format considerations that you should be watching for and heed. They are general rules of thumb to be used in the absence of specific directions in the RFP on how the grant application should be properly formatted.

- ☐ Margins are fully justified or straight on each side.
- ☐ All major section headings and subheadings are bold. Limit the use of boldface type elsewhere.
- ☐ Project title uses italics within text, without bolds.
- ☐ The proposal has a uniform appearance. (Be careful when photocopying to keep pages squared up.)
- ☐ Spacing is consistent throughout the proposal.
- ☐ The font is 12 pt. Times New Roman or Arial, and properly spaced.
- ☐ A high quality paper, printer, and/or copier are used.

## Step Four: Alternative Funding

☐ Paragraphs are equally spaced, with no indentions.

☐ One section follows the other without page breaks.

☐ Pages are centered and numbered at the bottom, and the page number indicates the total number of pages in the proposal (i.e. page 4 of 36).

☐ Limit the amount of underlining to avoid busy pages.

☐ When using bullets, there is a space between the bulleted items and the text.

☐ Margins are 1" unless otherwise specified.

☐ The proposal meets page requirements.

☐ The computer spell check has been used

☐ At least two other people have reviewed the proposal to check for errors.

☐ The format follows RFP specifications.

☐ All forms required by the RFP are completed.

☐ All signatures are present on forms.

☐ Double check instructions against forms.

☐ Include at least one original form, with original signatures in blue ink.

☐ Mark original copy with a removable note when submitting.

☐ Number all pages from beginning to end.

☐ Avoid the use of colored papers.

---

Key Point #12 - Failure to follow the RFPS formatting rules is a reason to reject your application. The number one reason grants are rejected is failure to follow instructions. The logic here is that if you cannot follow the simple instructions on how to organize and submit your proposal; how likely are you to follow the instructions if you have $100,000 of their money in your hands. See the point?

No No

---

The other important reason for following proper formatting is that this can be a reason for them to reject your grant prior to anyone ever reading it's content It isn't unusual to see 20K applications for a major Federal grant program and they simply must have some way to screen those applications so they do not have to read all of them. Reading 20K proposals would pose a logistical nightmare of gargantuan proportions for a funding source and nobody would ever see an award come out within a timely period after submission if they had to read all 20K applications.. Formatting is one of those things they can use to quickly screen out those applications that they will not have to read or score. Don't let yourself fall victim to this screening technique! Follow the RFPs directions, implicitly!

www.HDGrants.com     177

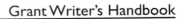

# 7. GRANT WRITING TIPS

**Writing Tips from Grant Experts at DHS, DHHS and DoJ**

Problem Section

Be specific – don't exaggerate or be vague.

Demonstrate the need for your methodology.

Ensure that reviewers can anticipate your solution based on your analysis of the problem.

Methods (Procedures) Section

Start with your objective and set out the precise steps you will take to achieve it.

Include what will be done, who will do it and when it will be done.

Explain what additional resources will be needed, how they will be paid for and how they will help you achieve your objective.

Evaluation Section

Include an evaluation component for every project objective.

Explain the methodologies to be used to validate the evaluation.

Stress evaluation as a tool for replicating the project in other programs.

Budget Section

Make sure your calculations are clear, logical and error-free.

Be comprehensive and include all associated costs — training, insurance, maintenance, etc.

Be specific, give details.

Include the cost of budget support.

Justify out of the ordinary expenditures even if not asked to do so.

## Ten Tips for Successful Grant Writing from the experts.

(These tips are the collected thoughts from senior evaluators at the Department of Health, Department of Justice and the Department of Health and Human Services)

1. ALWAYS FOLLOW DIRECTIONS!

2. Research the grant thoroughly.

**Grant Writer's Handbook**

3. Involve all other interested parties.

4. Establish credibility from the outset by initiating a dialog with the grant provider.

5. Be positive —know what the problem is, and what it takes to solve it.

6. Always have several people with different backgrounds and fields of expertise review your application and the math.

7. Make sure the proposal clearly explains the need, objections and solution.

8. Always comply with length restrictions imposed by the funding agency.

9. Make sure all elements of the proposal mesh together — goals and objectives must relate to the need/problem, activities must relate to objectives and so on.

10. Make sure it is submitted on time.

### Ten Reasons Why Grant Applicants Fail

Checklist
- ☐ Don't follow directions.
- ☐ Request too many items.
- ☐ Do not itemize costs.
- ☐ Fail to make a case for cost-benefit.
- ☐ Don't provide a problem statement.
- ☐ Don't shop around for lowest costs.
- ☐ Don't make a case for financial need.
- ☐ Don't check their work.
- ☐ Lack collaboration, partnerships.
- ☐ Request is for low priority items.

Source: Compiled by US Fire Administration and the Office for Domestic Preparedness

### Department of Justice

Grant evaluators at DOJ's Office of Justice Programs (OJP) recommend that grants writers follow a two step preparatory approach to ensure successful submissions.

The first step is planning – review the grant application notice, establish timetables, address the selection criteria and highlight model proposal strengths.

## Grant Writing Tips

Second, read the notice thoroughly and don't be intimidated by the language. Note any application workshops, print out all included forms and when in doubt, ask questions.

### *Ten questions to ask*

- ☐ Who is eligible?
- ☐ When is the deadline?
- ☐ What is the Catalog of Federal Domestic Assistance (CFDA) number?
- ☐ What is the award amount per grant?
- ☐ How many projects will be funded?
- ☐ Is there a matching requirement?
- ☐ Where can I get the application?
- ☐ Is there a page limit?
- ☐ Where do I submit the application?
- ☐ Who is the program contact?

The secret to successful grant writing, according to senior federal evaluators, is planning:

- ☐ Assess time available
- ☐ Research programs well in advance
- ☐ Spend two-thirds of your time on planning and one third on writing

Main reasons why applications are delayed or rejected:

- ☐ NOT clear or not detailed enough
- ☐ NOT consistent with institutional policy
- ☐ DOES NOT meet federal requirement
- ☐ NOT aligned with purpose or statute
- ☐ DOES NOT plot out the life of the grant, and
- ☐ DOES NOT achieve project goals

### *Useful tips from OJP evaluators:*

Use visual aids (charts, maps and tables) to emphasize main points and allow for quick comparison

Use most recent information and facts to establish need for the project, use Census data, compare target area with region and nation

www.HDGrants.com

181

Budget for the life of the grant, address matching requirements and nonfederal support from applicant and partners — community buy in

Above all, apply — you won't get anything if you don't apply!

The Department of Justice Response Center provides assistance and answers inquiries from the public, law enforcement agencies, institutions, and grantees about grants and programs, funding opportunities, and grant-management related questions. It provides application kits and assistance for grants available from the Office of Community Oriented Policing Services (COPS) and from the Office of Justice Programs (OJP), which includes the Bureau of Justice Assistance (BJA), Bureau of Justice Statistics (BJS), National Institute of Justice (NIJ), Office of Juvenile Justice and Delinquency Prevention (OJJDP), and Office for Victims of Crime (OVC). Person to person assistance is available from 9 a.m. to 5 p.m. (EST) Monday – Friday. Messages may be left after hours and calls will be returned the next business day. A 24-hour fax-on-demand service is also available.

# 8. Step Five: After the Application Process

## "Congratulations, Your Grant Is Approved"

These five words are what you have worked so hard for, and we sincerely hope that you hear them! However, keep in mind that you haven't officially been awarded a grant until you have the actual award notification letter in hand. You should not take any actions towards purchasing items, implementing the program or moving forward with the project until you have received an official award letter. To do so, would mean that those expenditures could be considered as pre-award expenses and therefore not eligible for use of grant funds to reimburse. You should also not make any formal announcements to the press or in official meetings until such time as the award letter is in hand. There can sometimes be precursory inquiries and actions that would indicate that an award is pending or that you will be receiving an award but, it is not official until you have the letter saying so. Be cautious! Resist doing anything until you are sure you have the award.

Remember

It is a good idea not to combine grant funds with other funding, so that proper tracking of the funding can occur. There are also provisions on some grants that prohibit you from putting these funds into interest bearing accounts or comingling them with other funds. Your best practice here? Have a separate account at your bank where all grant money goes and is subsequently tracked.

No No

Be sure you check on these requirements, too.

### Don't Stumble and Fall

What do you do now that you have the money? Simple; you do what you said you were going to do in the grant application. In the application, you stated exactly what you were going to do with the money, when you were going to do it and what the results would be.

When you receive notice that the funds have been awarded to you, start following your local procurement policies and obtain the bids for the equipment.

Tips

A few words of caution are needed here in regards to Procurement Integrity with Federal Grant Award money:

Sole source providing is frowned upon highly by the government

www.HDGrants.com

### Grant Writer's Handbook

Recent interpretations of CFR44 13.36, which controls procurement policies with Federal grant funding, need to be thoroughly read and followed.

The government is strictly enforcing those policies to the extent that program guidance and RFP documents of late, have entire new sections of language devoted to this subject. They are not taking this lightly and violations of same can result in retraction of an award and investigation by the US Attorney General's Office and OMB. Something you do not want to happen.

The problem is a non-competitive bid proposal being submitted. Be overly cautious in this area as during routine audits or inspections the procedure you followed in securing bids will be scrutinized!

As you begin this process, you are starting into the phase of grant strategy known as grant administration and management. This is where a large number of departments stumble and fall.

### How Do I Get The Money?

It depends on the grantor. With most Federal grant programs, you will have a direct deposit into your account. You may also have to request a drawdown of funds or present invoices or billing statements before they will transfer the money to your account. If you have options as to how you will receive the funds, always choose the drawdown option. This will save you time if you ever face an audit.

### Document, Document, Document

Must Do

Key Point #13 - You must keep proper documentation of every dime that you spend, establishing a clear and accurate paper trail. OMB Circular A-133 clearly states that any recipient of Federal funding is subject to a Federal audit of their entire grant program. They can scrutinize every aspect of your program, including checking the numbers that you put in the grant application, making sure you followed proper purchasing and bidding procedures, verifying that you accepted the right bids, tracked and maintained the bank records and achieved the goals and objectives that you stated in your grant application.

So, document everything that you do with Federal grant funds. You do not want a Federal auditor to file a negative report. – that could undermine your future chances of obtaining additional funds. Remember, if you did not document it, it never happened.

From the very beginning, you should keep everything on file. Copy everything — research you did, statistical data, bid sheets, cancelled checks. Keep it handy and in a safe place.

## Step Five: After The Application Process

Most Federal grants have a three years-after performance period records retention clause. Your best practice here, which has been proven time and time again is to follow these instruction.

Tips

Key Point #14 - Start keeping a file from the moment you start researching a grant and everything, and I mean everything, about that grant goes into that fie. Research, statistical sources, reports used, cancelled checks, email correspondence, phone logs, receipts, bid specs, packing slips, invoices and all. A copy of the grant application, award documents etc, letters of support all will go in here as well. Everything gets copied and put in the file before going to other places where it may be required. A large manila envelope can serve this purpose well.

When the grants' period of performance is over, obtain a large 3-ring binder, clear protective sheets, index tabs and then categorize everything that you have saved into certain sections like correspondence, invoices, application, financials, bid specs and bid awards. Then put everything in the protective sheet holders, file under the correct index tabs and then label the binder and put in a safe accessible place. If and when a Grant Management Specialist shows up to audit or examine your records you will simply have to hand them one book with everything in it. The last thing in the world you want is to have a GMS going on a fishing expedition in your city or department files searching for that one check you cannot find.

## Dates and Details

Remember

Key Point #15 - Stay in close contact with your grant program contact and grant manager. Periodic reports will be required of you, and these reports should never be late or incomplete. They are getting pretty sticky about this in the Federal grants right now and we are aware of departments who have had their awarded funding "locked" up till reports got filed. Mark your calendars with these dates and allow ample time to compile statistical data, or other relevant information that the reports may require of you, and get them filed on time.

The GMS (Grant Management System) tracks all of your Federal funding and the reports that should be filed with them. If you become delinquent in the reporting areas, you will not be allowed to file another application for funding until you get your reports caught up and it may cause you loss of points due to past performance issues on your part.

Remember

Do not forget about matching funds, either. Make sure that your budget has this money set aside. Again, document every dime you, or your agency, contributes. If the money is not there now, remember that sometimes, you have until the grant period ends (generally 12 months from the date of award) to show that your portion of the grant was in fact budgeted and spent towards that equipment. The program guidelines will tell you if this is allowed or not.

www.HDGrants.com

# Grant Writer's Handbook

Follow all draw-down or distribution directions to the letter. Do not deviate from the stated procedures.

### Spend It, Don't Return It!

**Must Do** — In most cases, there is a simple rule that you must always follow — never give money back! If they've taken the time to review your application and set money aside for you, then use it, just as you said you would.

That being said, you should always spend the money during the allotted time. One of the worst things you can do is to fail to properly expend funding given to you. The other thing to watch out for is receiving something and then failing to put it into use. You do not ever want to have a Grant Management Specialist come into your department and find items that you supposedly justified by saying " this is a safety issue with our employees" still boxed up and sitting on the pallet they were delivered on 6 months prior. Spec it, bid, it , receive it, issue it!

**No No** — If you said you were going to buy 15 items, then you need to buy those items. Most grant programs will have a program specialist visit your agency during the time the grant program is running. He or she will want to examine what you purchased and how you have been expending the money. It is like a mini- audit. This is a visit that you do not want to fail. Stay on top of your reports and spend that money.

**Must Do** — If you are having problems with a vendor, and their delivery dates, then advise the grantor of that status and keep them in the loop on what is happening with their money. You can quickly find yourself in default on your grant terms of award by not following through on this properly. Always keep the grantor advised of changes and obtain their guidance before making decisions affecting their money. If you sense a problem, correct your course quickly. Usually a quick amendment filed on behalf of your agency can correct any problem in its infancy instead of discovery during a full blown audit and having a finding placed against you.

**No No** — Key Point #16 - Finally, never, ever, spend grant money for purposes other than those originally stated in your grant. To do so is to commit fraud, and if you are dealing with a Federal grant program, it is a Federal offense.

You should also be prepared to cover yourself, your co-workers, and your superiors extensively via memos, emails, etc. As the grant contact person, you won't necessarily be held accountable for misuse of funds authorized by your superiors, but as a matter of integrity, you should be prepared to make them fully aware of the potential consequences of their decisions. Part of your job description as the grants management person for your agency is to advise them of potential problems or conflicts with the grant funding sources priorities. Take that responsibility seriously.

## Step Five: After The Application Process

*"Hey, I Have Money Left Over. Can I Spend This Too?"*

The simple answer to that question is "yes," but not without gaining permission first. Most grant RFPs will clearly state what excess funds may be used for, and in what amounts.

For instance, the Assistance to Firefighters Grant states, "You may spend up to $5,000 of excess money on additional equipment that furthers the scope of your project (It would not pay for you to buy "extras or spares" ). Anything in excess of $5,000 must be spent on Fire Prevention and Education activities or returned to FEMA."

The key here is that they encourage you to be cost wise. In most cases, you will be rewarded for that type of activity by being allowed to obtain additional equipment that you had not asked for. Call your program grant manager, tell them what is going on, and follow their directions. Remember when having phone conversations to keep a record of who you talked to and when. It is a good idea to follow up any phone conversation with a confirming email and file it with the reply.

### Good PR

It is perfectly normal to want to bask in the glow of receiving your award for a little while. Let the local public know what you did and how you are saving them tax-dollars. Try to arrange a photo op where your local Congressional representative presents you with a large facsimile check. This also shows the public that you are utilizing programs to help keep taxes stable and may alert the public to growing concerns or problems that your department is facing. This is all good public relations and gives your department a chance to enjoy the positive media coverage you need.

Remember

### Receiving the dreaded "Dear John" Letter

You have been sitting on pins and needles for three months now, waiting to hear if your grant was funded. The letter finally arrives from the funding source and….. the news is bad — you have been declined. These are commonly referred to as "DJ notices or Dear Johns.

Just remember that you have only lost a battle, not the war. Competition for grant money is fierce, so you are not the only department reading the bad news. There will always be winners and losers in every program. A good grant writer in this country averages winning 1 out of 6 grants they write. Look at rejection as just being one step closer to a win. There are other methods, funding sources and alternatives.

The important thing is not to let one defeat cause you to quit the grants game. You'll do better next time. If it is any consolation at all, it took this author almost three years to finally crack the code and get a grant

Remember

www.HDGrants.com

187

## Grant Writer's Handbook

award and that was only as a result of my co-author's assistance at that time!. Stay in this business for long and a Dear John letter will find its way to your desk, trust me.

### Learn From Your Mistakes

Government agencies and the private sector are notoriously famous for just sending a form letter of denial. They may, or may not, tell you in the letter what you did wrong or why they refused to fund your project.

Sometimes you have to read between the lines, paying attention to subtle details. Look for clues, like "your program does not meet our current criteria." A message like this means you have failed to address the funding source's key priorities. Another common form letter phrase is " although your grant application was good, the reviewer's did not feel that your financial need was compelling enough to merit an award". Well, go look at that financial needs section again; something was missing. Go back over the original RFP (Request for Proposal) or NOFA (Notice of Funding Availability) and critique yourself on addressing those priorities and particular areas if mentioned.

Sometimes you can tell by the date you received the letter. In 2009, if you had received a rejection letter from FEMA regarding the Assistance to Firefighters Grant Program by September 15, your grant never made it through the initial computer scoring process. That means it was not considered to be "competitive." It also means a human being never read it!

Examine the numbers you put into the questions at the beginning of the application process. Many departments we've talked to that received rejection notices had, inadvertently, contradicted themselves by placing a zero in the "number of firefighter injuries" column when the grant's main stated priority was to "prevent firefighter injuries and increase firefighter safety." Too many Chiefs were worried that their Workman's Comp insurance would go up if they reported their actual injuries, no matter how minor they were. In this particular instance, failure to show any injuries hurt their chances for funding from a source that had firefighter safety as a primary objective. The Workman's Comp issue was actually a non-issue since they weren't the ones reading the grant application.

If you have a friend at the Federal or State level in one of the funding offices, call him or her for feedback on what you did wrong. Honor their confidentiality and take what they tell you to heart. Remember, they have no reason to withhold grant money; it's their job to give it away.

It may also be exactly the right time to seek the assistance of a professional grant consultant. Having someone give your grant an unbiased, objective review can be very

## Step Five: After The Application Process

enlightening. Of course the logical thing to do is to have a professional review your work PRIOR to submission where their comments and or editing can help your grant application immensely. The cost for this is completely justifiable and reasonable in most circumstances when you consider what may be at stake. It is not unusual to realize a 100:1 or higher return on investment to a department utilizing reviewing service prior to submission. It saves time and in most cases results in a positive outcome.

### Persistence

There is always more than one funding source, and there are always other grants for which you can apply.

*Remember*

Rejection of your grant by one funding source does not necessarily mean it will be rejected by another. It may simply be that the funding source just ran out of money!

Let's face it, when you have 8,500 grants to give away and 22,500 agencies apply for them, someone has to win, and someone has to lose. "No" does not mean never. It simply means, "Not right now. So, try again!"

We have seen grant applications rejected two or three times and then get funded on the fourth try, without a word on the grant application ever being changed. This happens simply through attrition; people with more need are being funded ahead of you and it has taken that long to rise to the top.

Don't give up. Try and try again. Even a professional grant writer receives rejection notices — and they do it for a living!

*Tips*

### Critique the Application

Give a couple of copies of your rejected grant to a few others in your community. Do not give it to another officer in your department or your city manager. Give it to the local high school English teacher or that friend of yours who is a bank official. Have a professional look at it before you submit it. The payment of a small reasonable fee that results in catching a major mistake that costs you a $250,000 grant, is always money well spent. Ask their opinions and listen to what they tell you. We highly recommend you do this before you submit the grant. If you didn't do this originally, now is a good time to start.

Keep an open mind about what they are telling you. Maybe your language or explanations were too technical, or they could not understand your jargon. Maybe you did not paint a clear enough picture of the department's financial need.

www.HDGrants.com                                                                                                                                    189

Grant Writer's Handbook

Remember — Rejection is a hard pill for anyone to swallow. Too many walk away after being rejected, and this is simply the wrong tactic to use. Get over it, and get on with it! Adapt, improvise, and overcome! The effort you expend will eventually pay off.

## *Checklist Of Common Reasons Grants Get Declined*

Grant proposal writing is a highly competitive undertaking. The number of proposals submitted and requested dollars far exceeds available funding from all sources. The general rule of thumb is that 80% of all proposals submitted fail. Bad proposals should fail but many excellent proposals also fail to make the funding line.

Why? There are many reasons ranging from the most obvious to the most arcane and subjective. Some of the more obvious reasons that grant proposals get rejected are due to any one or a combination of the following.

Applying the following checklist to your grant BEFORE you send it will significantly decrease the number of times that you receive rejections notices.

### 1. Failure to Follow Directions

Checklist — You failed to follow one or more of the submittal requirements
- ☐ You failed to address one or more of the evaluation criteria
- ☐ Read the information thoroughly. Go to the workshops. Read and highlight the guidelines in the RFP.
- ☐ Pay attention to deadlines as well as how the grant application has to arrive and where.
- ☐ Use proper formatting as stated and do not exceed page limitations.
- ☐ Your proposal failed to adequately address the funding source rationale for making the funds available
- ☐ Your project activities are not eligible for funding source approval
- ☐ Your proposal is submitted to a funding source that does not match your giving interest or client focus
- ☐ Your proposed project is judged infeasible on legal or technical grounds
- ☐ You simply cannot write
- ☐ You simply cannot follow basic instructions for writing, assembling and submitting a grant proposal
- ☐ One or more of your required proposal components was judged weak or non-responsive

### 2. Requesting Too Many Items

- ☐ No "shopping cart" approach. Remember "needy, not greedy!"
- ☐ The items you request should be in line with the size of your department and your service area.
- ☐ It is advisable to keep the number of items to 3-4 per application. If you must, break the program up into phases and complete it as such, with several grants.

## Step Five: After The Application Process

- Remember that for every item you seek to obtain, you must thoroughly justify that expenditure. If you have too many items, you will have to weaken the justification of each in order to stay within word count or page limitations. Better to strongly justify 3- 4 items, and win them, than to try and justify 8 items and do a poor job at justifying each of them and risk losing the entire grant as a result.

### 3. Incomplete Budget

- Your budget or budget narrative was unrealistic or incomplete
- Figures don't add up
- If you request equipment, make sure you shop for the best price. Then spell it out clearly: 10 So many units at $???? for a total cost of $??????.
- Don't forget about training costs.
- Administrative and audit costs.
- Travel costs to attend training or to take delivery of equipment.
- Shipping costs.
- Service and maintenance costs or extended warranties.

### 4. Not Making Your Case On A Cost-Benefit Basis

- You must show that the dollars expended produce the largest benefit to your agency and to the surrounding community. Remember to address the "triumvirate" of us, we, and them.
- It is imperative to include mutual aid situations and interagency cooperation. Include the other agencies in your plans, and show that your receipt of the equipment helps other jurisdictions and the community at large.
- Biggest Bang for the Buck!

### 5. You Didn't Provide An Adequate Problem Description

- You have to provide a "state of the community and my department" statement.
- Describe in detail why you are having the problem.
- Who, What, When, Where and Why
- You are an artist painting a picture with words; you must immerse the reviewer into your community and its problems. Make the reviewer see the problem through your eyes but always bear in mind that the reviewer is "blind" and you must provide that detail and descriptive information in your words that you choose.
- Your proposal was viewed by the readers as incoherent or un-convincing
- Your proposal problem is too ambitious relative to the ability of your organization to have a favorable impact on the problem or need you stated in your proposal

### 6. You Didn't Shop Around For The Lowest Prices

- The Federal minimum guideline says that you should obtain two quotes. Remember to follow your local procurement policies and procedures implicitly, no short cuts.
- Don't ask for a Cadillac if a VW will do the job.

www.HDGrants.com

Grant Writer's Handbook

☐ Reviewer's hate "greedy" departments. If you raise the "greedy flag," you will be denied or rejected. The request must be reasonable for your department and the problem you are asking for assistance with.

### 7. Not Making A Compelling Case Of Financial Need

☐ You have to make a strong argument that you cannot afford to fund this activity (e.g., tax referendums were defeated, businesses moved out, bad crop years, etc.) State what funding events you tried and what success levels you attained, or did not attain. If you have applied before, say that you have done so and that although you have not been able to budget it in, you still have a great need for the equipment.

☐ Keep your request in line with your agency size, personnel, and the community you service.

☐ They must know you are attempting to handle the problem yourselves, but are not able to keep pace.

☐ Your proposal failed to clearly demonstrate a need for the funding

### 8. Failing To Check Your Work In The Document

☐ Do all your figures agree?

☐ Have you left out an important detail?

☐ Do you have spelling errors?

☐ Have it proofread professionally before you push the submit button.

### 9. The Grant Fails To Encourage Collaborative Efforts And Interagency Cooperation

☐ Make sure you include this element in your grant. It will give you higher scores.

☐ Place the header or sub header "Interagency Interoperability" so it gets noticed.

☐ Show that the stakeholders were involved in the process or that their concerns are being addressed.

☐ Prove that you are a team player and that your agencies around you can all "play together well in the same sandbox", so to speak.

### 10. You Requested Items Which Are Low Priority

☐ Request items specifically stated to be receiving a high priority and stay away from the lower priority items.

☐ Mixing higher priorities with lower priorities lowers your total overall score.

☐ Grants are often decided by as little as 0.25% of a single point.

### 11. They Ran Out Of Money!

☐ Too many applicants.

☐ Not enough funding.

If you feel there is nothing wrong with your application, update it and resubmit next year. . Many times by simple attrition, your grant will rise to the top as more needy departments ahead of you are funded.

## Step Five: After The Application Process

Tips

Applying a checklist to your grant BEFORE you send it will significantly decrease the number of times that you receive rejections notices.

As you look over this list of rejection factors, some of them sound harsh and even unbelievable. But after more than 20 years of writing, reading and funding thousands of proposals, experience tells me that these and more are true. Grant proposal writing is a harsh and unforgiving enterprise.

Remember

To succeed in the grant writing arena you must have elephant skin, a tolerance for constant rejection amid notable success; a mind for creative conceptualization within the context of a group; and the ability to absorb details while assembling and submitting proposals correctly.

Finally, grant writers cannot be lone wolfs. Proposals are written from within an organization to resolve problems that are defined in part by the organization's leadership and the people they serve. These organizational needs and problems must be matched to funding sources that have more than a passing interest in what your organization is seeking to accomplish.

Remember

It is important to remember that once awarded, a grant does something to you as well as for you. An organization's management must not allow a grant writer to write grants that will have a negative impact on the organization's mission, priorities, or business practices. What good does it do to win a grant if its purposes or activities are likely to invite dissention or controversy? What good is achieved by a proposal that will cause you to take on other commitments that you are not prepared to assume?

### Submittal Requirements

All grants from the simplest to the most complex have assembly and submittal requirements. There are page limitations that may or may not include the forms as part of the page count. There are instructions on things like margins and font size. Ignore them at you absolute peril! Deadlines are important and they are expressed in two ways. Most deadlines are stated as "received by" which means that your proposal must arrive on or before the date and time stated. Late proposals are automatically rejected. Some funding sources specify a "mailed by" deadline which means that your proposal must be postmarked or date-stamped by a time certain with the evidence visible on the sent package.

### Evaluation Criteria

Most proposal invitations have some statement of criteria that the funding source will use to judge the merit of your proposal. In complex proposal invitations, these criteria are

# Grant Writer's Handbook

usually separately stated in the funding announcement or a regulatory document when it is a government that invites you proposal. Your proposal must demonstrate that you have considered and addressed the evaluation criteria. These evaluation criteria are usually expressed in terms of agency needs or priorities and proposal outcomes that should be reflected in your proposal narrative.

## Proposal Components

No No

Every grant-giver that invites proposals for funding consideration will have a required list of components that must be reflected in your proposal narrative. A fully responsive proposal must reflect each required proposal component even if you have some discretion to add non-required components to the proposal. If you leave out a critical component or address that component very weakly, your proposal will suffer in the ratings. A seriously deficient proposal will be rejected.

## Budget Issues

Most proposal readers will conclude that if you can't do the numbers, you cannot do anything else. The budget is usually worth 10-20% of your total score. However, if the numbers do not make sense, are incorrect or your budget us incomplete, the result is almost always fatal to proposal success. Not only must your line item budget and forms match up but your budget must clearly relate to your proposed activities.

## Funding Source Rationale

Grant-givers give money for particular reasons. They want to promote change, advance a particular policy, or entice you to address a national problem in a particular way. Whatever the rationale for making the funds available, your proposal must demonstrate that the funding source's objectives are being advanced. You must show how the funding source and its clients will benefit by funding your proposal.

## Addressing the Need

Remember

A good need statement is supported by a combination of hard and soft data. Hard data denotes statistical information in national, regional, and local context. Soft data consists of testimonials and vivid stories that help the reader understand the human and emotional context of your need that statistics cannot convey.

## Your Unique Selling Proposition

When you apply for a grant to resolve a problem or address a particular need, a funding source is likely to wonder, why they should fund you as opposed to some other organization that is also seeking funding. If there is something that is unique about your organization or key

194        www.HDGrants.com

## Step Five: After The Application Process

staff that makes you uniquely qualified to achieve uncommon results, you need to articulate what that is to the funding source.

### Problem Definition and Scope

How you define your problem and its scope can substantially affect your chances of being funded. If you define your problem too broadly the funding source may rightly conclude that your proposal is too ambitious or that your problem is incapable of resolution. If your problem is defined too narrowly, the funding source may conclude that the impact of your proposal will be minimal. If you define your problem in a manner that is not readily apparent to the reader, the funding source may conclude that your proposal lacks focus.

### Project Approach and Activities

Even if you have clearly articulated a need for funding or set forth a clearly defined problem, your proposal may still fail if your proposed approach or activities are inappropriate. Your approach or methods used for resolving an identified problem must be realistic and workable. For example, if your problem targets drug prevention among a low income minority population and your strategy or approach to reaching the target population is unrealistic, you risk rejection of your proposal. Likewise, if your actual activities are ineligible for funding consideration or do not directly relate to addressing the needs of your proposed beneficiaries, your proposal will be judged unrealistic.

### Project Infeasibility

Even when you have demonstrated a particular need and the qualifications to address the need, your project approach, and activities must be feasible. Watch out for activities that may have a negative impact or be ineligible for legal reasons. For example, a federal or state agency may not fund projects that will have a serious negative impact on the environment unless your activities are accompanied by a mitigation plan. Another example is a proposal that seeks to protect a group's civil rights through litigation against the government. Such proposals are excluded by law or regulation.

Another example is proposing to build a "white elephant". Asking to build a 100,000 square foot building for a fire station in a tiny rural town is unrealistic. Besides that, how will you pay the operation and maintenance costs on such a large structure with few residents or other users to pay for its upkeep?

## The Wrong Funding Source

 Key Point #17 - It makes no sense to seek funding from a funding source that does not give to your area of focus, does not fund the activities you desire to fund, or does not grant to your type of organization. But careless research and pre-qualification techniques are the main reasons that many grant-givers receive inappropriate proposals.

## Problems With The Proposal Writing and Structure

If you are good at articulating your funding concept but cannot write well, find or hire a good grant writer. Taken as a whole, your proposal must be coherent. It must hang together, flow naturally, and convince the reader. Before you submit your proposal, have others not involved in its writing read it. If they have many questions or do not understand it, revise the proposal to address logical, structural and grammar weaknesses.

Even if the required proposal components seem illogical or irrational, you must still include them in your proposal. You may have to provide for special transitions or other explanations or cross-references, but this is preferable to going your own way. Remember, the funding source is giving the money. Sometimes a seriously flawed proposal structure is released. You are within your rights to seek clarification about the content and structure of the proposal prior to its submission. Funding sources have been known to amend grant solicitations that are seriously flawed.

## Analyze the Funding Opportunity and develop a Requirements Checklist

Is there some way to anticipate or avoid many of these problems in the first place? Sure. Take time to carefully review the funding solicitation. Read it several times so that you understand it as a whole and all of its components. Now make a checklist of submittal and assembly requirements and a checklist of required proposal components. These checklists will help ensure that you address all of the narrative requirements and all of the assembly and submittal requirements.

# 9. Wrap Up

Getting into the grants ballgame is a wise decision. It is an endeavor that more public safety agencies need to utilize, in their constant struggle to fund their departments. You have taken a huge step in the right direction by advancing your education in this process.

We hope that you have found this book to be of assistance in understanding the process and in actually constructing your grant proposal. Remember, our assistance to you does not need to end when you finish reading this manual.

Homeland Defense - Grants is a full service grant consulting firm. Our services as consultants are available to you. It is our desire to be your grant information "go to" source. To that end, we pledge to continue in our efforts and to improve that service wherever possible.

When you need financial backup, just pick up the phone and call us or send us an e-mail with your questions and concerns. We will always give you the best information that is available. Plus, we can assist you with:

- ☐ Grant reviewing prior to submission
- ☐ Grant Writing
- ☐ Project Development
- ☐ Grant Management Services
- ☐ Grants Related Research
- ☐ Procurement and Bid Writing
- ☐ Grant training seminars
- ☐ Corporate Staff Training
- ☐ Agency hosted seminars
- ☐ Speaking engagements
- ☐ Funding source location
- ☐ Alternative fundraising ideas

www.HDGrants.com

Homeland Defense Grants thanks you for your interest and we hope that you will continue to pursue grants as a supplementary source of funding for your agency. If we may assist you in that process, please feel free to contact us.

Homeland Defense –Grants

5372 Sandhamn Ln., Second Floor

Longboat Key, Fl. 34228

Office 941-752-5757

www.HDGrants.com

# Notes

# Notes

Grant Writer's Handbook